# KT-132-146

By the same author in Pan Books

THE RISE OF HENRY MORCAR

INHERITANCE

THE BRONTËS

Phyllis Bentley, who lives in Yorkshire, was educated at Cheltenham Ladies' College and Leeds University. She is the author of eighteen novels, which have been widely published; these include *Inheritance*, *Love and Money* and *The Rise of Henry Morcar*. She is also the author of another distinguished work, *The Brontës and Their World*.

THE BRONTËS

PHYLLIS BENTLEY

PAN BOOKS LTD : LONDON

First published 1947 by Home & Van Thal Ltd
Second edition published 1966 by Arthur Barker Ltd
This edition published 1973 by Pan Books Ltd,
33 Tothill Street, London SW1

ISBN 0 330 23882 5

Printed in Great Britain by
Cox & Wyman Ltd, London, Reading and Fakenham

The
Yorkshire Television
production of

THE BRONTËS OF HAWARTH

by Christopher Fry

Alfred Burke	—	The Rev Patrick Brontë
Michael Kitchen	—	Branwell Brontë
Vickery Turner	—	Charlotte Brontë
Rosemary McHale	—	Emily Brontë
Ann Penfold	—	Anne Brontë

and

Barbara Leigh Hunt as the Narrator, Mrs Gaskell

Executive Producer
PETER WILLES

Produced and Directed by
MARC MILLER

CONTENTS

LIST OF ILLUSTRATIONS

(between pages 52 and 53)

BIOGRAPHICAL DATES

1777	Patrick Brontë born in County Down, Ireland.
1783	Maria Branwell born in Cornwall.
1802–6	Patrick Brontë at Cambridge University.
1809	Rev Patrick Brontë takes a curacy in Yorkshire.
1812	Maria Branwell stays with relations in Yorkshire. Rev P. Brontë and Maria Branwell marry.
1813	Maria Brontë born.
1815	Elizabeth Brontë born.
1816	Charlotte Brontë born.
1817	Patrick Branwell Brontë born.
1818	Emily Jane Brontë born.
1820	Anne Brontë born. The Brontës remove to Haworth.
1821	Mrs Brontë dies.
1822	Miss Branwell comes to Haworth.
1824	Maria, Elizabeth, Charlotte and Emily at Cowan Bridge School.
1825	Maria and Elizabeth die. Charlotte and Emily return home.
1826–7	The plays *Young Men*, *Our Fellows* and *Islanders*, origins of Angria and Gondal, established.
1831–2	Charlotte at school at Roe Head, Mirfield.
1835	Charlotte returns to Roe Head as governess. Emily spends three months at Roe Head, when she returns home and Anne takes her place. Branwell visits London
1836	Emily is governess at Law Hill school, Halifax, for six months.
1839	Charlotte and Anne take their first situations as governesses in private families.

1840	Rev William Weightman at Haworth. Charlotte and Emily at Haworth. Anne away as governess.
1841	Charlotte takes her second situation as governess in private house. Anne becomes governess at Thorp Green.
1842 *Feb*	Charlotte and Emily go as pupils to the Pensionnat Heger, Brussels.
Oct	Rev W. Weightman dies. Miss Branwell dies.
Nov	Charlotte and Emily return to Haworth.
Dec	Branwell goes as tutor to Thorp Green.
1843 *Jan*	Charlotte returns to Pensionnat Heger as governess.
1844	Charlotte returns to Haworth. Rev A. B. Nicholls comes to Haworth.
1845	Branwell dismissed from Thorp Green.
1846	*Poems by Currer, Ellis and Acton Bell* published. Charlotte takes Rev P. Brontë to have cataract operation in Manchester. She begins to write *Jane Eyre* there.
1847 *Oct*	*Jane Eyre* published.
Dec	*Wuthering Heights* and *Agnes Grey* published.
1848 *July*	Charlotte and Anne visit London. *The Tenant of Wildfell Hall* published.
Sept	Branwell dies.
Dec	Emily dies.
1849 *May*	Anne dies at Scarborough.
	Shirley published.
1849 & 1850	Charlotte visits London and the Lakes, and makes literary friends, including Mrs Gaskell. Richmond draws her portrait.
1851	James Taylor goes to India.
1853	*Villette* published.

CHAPTER I

The Brontës' Materials and Equipment

INTRODUCTION

THE contribution made by the three Brontë sisters to English literature has a unique flavour – a strange pungent mingling of wild romance and domestic realism, of cosmic poetry and local detail, quite personal and peculiar. They derive from no previous 'school' nor have any succeeding writers produced work of similar tang. This originality, which gives them a just claim to be considered major English writers, is definitely traceable to certain circumstances of their lives, of which the elements are perhaps not unusual in themselves, but highly singular as regards their combination. A study of these circumstances as the source of their equipment and materials is an essential preliminary to any true understanding of the Brontës' work.

CELTIC

The first of these circumstances is their heredity.

Their father, Patrick Brontë or Brunty or Prunty – the

point is undetermined though his children did not know
this – was an Irishman, born in Emdale in the southern
division of County Down, on St Patrick's Day 1777. He
was the eldest son of Hugh Brontë, who at that time probably farmed a few acres of land. Hugh was a Protestant, his
wife, Alice, a Catholic. This mixed parentage, uncomfortable in Ulster, may have helped to turn Patrick's thoughts
to leaving Ireland. In all, Hugh and Alice had ten children,
who seem, by the legends told of their wild doings, to have
been notably handsome and of strong personality. Some of
their descendants live in the district to this day; I had the
pleasure of seeing one of them, a young man, when I visited
Emdale in 1932; strangely enough he had something of the
same dark red hair, prominent nose and flashing eye as
descriptions and portraits give to Patrick Brontë's son
Branwell.

Emdale lies in the heart of a series of gently rolling hills.
The country has all the usual North Ireland characteristics:
it is divided into many small fields, given up chiefly to oats
and pasture; the usual rich Irish hedges, with their honey-
suckles and fuchsias and briers, border the lanes; cattle
stand about peacefully in the green, the very green, grass;
a few sheep crop the hillside among the branching thistles.
Away on the horizon, between the gentle curves of the near
hills, tower the Mountains of Mourne, dark blue, jagged,
sombre. Barefooted, ragged Irish children such as Patrick
Brontë was at eight or ten years old run along the rough
lanes, and the soft Irish air, with its eternal wistful melancholy, blows over all. The cottage in which Patrick was
born (now respectfully restored) was by 1932 reduced to
part of two walls with a mound of nettle-covered masonry

between; when intact it would have been a white-washed cabin, some twenty feet by twenty-five. Hugh Brontë prospered later and built himself a better house, but the cabin where Patrick was born was the home of a peasant, a poor man.

Patrick is said to have been both blacksmith and weaver of linen during his youth, but by the time he was sixteen he was already schoolmaster of a little village school. From there he passed on to be tutor in the family of the vicar of neighbouring Drumballyroney, the Rev Mr Tighe, who in return perhaps coached the promising lad, certainly set him on the road which led to Cambridge. The ability must have been brilliant indeed which in 1802 brought a bare-footed gossoon from remote Emdale to a sizarship at St John's. In 1806 Patrick took his degree, was ordained, and secured a curacy in Essex; in 1809 through a curate friend named Morgan he came to a curacy in Yorkshire, a county he never afterwards left as a residence. From this period onward Patrick showed himself quite a prolific author; he published in all two books of verse, two books in prose, three pamphlets and two sermons. From all accounts he was at this period handsome and sociable, even flirtatious, in disposition.

In 1812 Patrick married Maria Branwell, a Cornish gentlewoman lately orphaned, who had come from her home in Penzance to stay near Leeds with an uncle, John Fennell, who was in turn Methodist local preacher, head-master of a Wesleyan Academy and clergyman of the Established Church. Patrick's friend Morgan was engaged to Fennell's daughter; it was very natural that Patrick should fall in love with Miss Fennell's cousin, the small neat

Miss Branwell. Some of her love-letters to him are extant; they show a mind of sense and taste, an affectionate heart, a gentle humour and a flow of well-chosen words. At the time of their marriage Patrick was the incumbent of Hartshead near Dewsbury, and here his two children Maria and Elizabeth were born. In 1815 Patrick moved to Thornton, a little village west of Bradford, north-west of his previous home. At Thornton, Charlotte was born in 1816, Patrick Branwell in 1817, Emily Jane in 1818, and Anne in 1820.

The Brontë parents not only made the usual transmissions of heredity to their children, but by being what they were where they were created a peculiar mental climate in the children's home.

Patrick Brontë must have been an intensely ambitious man in his youth; he was a man who had come a long way up from very humble beginnings, who had raised himself entirely by his own mental ability and application. He valued the position of a clergyman of the Church of England perhaps rather more than a vicar to whom the status had come more easily – I think he valued it too highly to diminish it by any indiscriminate hobnobbing. He believed in reading, in education – look what they had done for him – and gladly sent his four elder little girls to the clergy school at Cowan Bridge where Maria and Elizabeth developed the consumption of which they died. Patrick was a strong Church and State man, passionately attached to the Church which had made his life, but not a mystic in religion. His wife on the other hand came of a Methodist family, strongly and fervently pious.

Both the Brontë parents had a certain literary ability. It

is true that Maria Branwell's only work written with a view
to print, an essay on *The Advantages of Poverty in Religious Concerns*, is trite though flowing; it is true that the
Reverend Patrick's poems are mostly quite excruciatingly
dull. But that the parents brought the literary tradition to
their family climate, so that their children grew up familiar
with the idea of writing for publication, is also true and
very important in the Brontë sisters' lives.

Both Brontë parents belonged to a race, or if that is too
strong an expression let us say a form of civilization,
definitely Celtic. Patrick was Irish, Maria came from that
Cornwall to which in early British history the Romans
drove the native British race. The Celts are a fluent people
compared with the tongue-tied Saxons; fluent and fiery,
restless and romantic, versatile and volatile, poetical and
proud. Whether Patrick, who according to Charlotte's
friend Ellen Nussey was an admirable raconteur, told his
children Celtic legends which actually moulded the structure and incidents of *Wuthering Heights* and *Jane Eyre*, we
cannot be sure, but at least he carried in his mind many
picturesque and wild Irish tales and in his veins Irish blood.

The Brontës in Yorkshire were strangers in a strange
land. Great-uncle Fennell and the Morgans were their only
relatives in northern England, and after their mother's
death in 1821 the tie of relationship seems to have become
rather slack. Patrick may or may not have kept up correspondence with his Irish relatives – the evidence is con-
flicting – but in either case they were far away. The little
Brontës had therefore no uncles and aunts near at hand, no
cousins with whom to play on equal terms, no single home
they could enter freely uninvited. This quite singular

loneliness, which moulded the Brontës' lives, characters and works, was accentuated by their father's appointment in 1820 to the incumbency of Haworth.

YORKSHIRE

Haworth has been much described by Brontë biographers, but perhaps too much in itself, too little in its relations to the outside world; it is not only Haworth alone but Haworth as part of the West Riding system which helped to mould the Brontë genius.

Rolling down the middle of England from north to south, from the Lake District in Cumberland to the Peak in Derbyshire, there stretches a range of interlocking hills now called the Pennine Chain. The geological character of this range varies; those hills of the West Riding amongst which Haworth stands are formed of sombre millstone grit. This dark millstone grit cannot grow rich crops or pasture; rough grass, a scanty crop of oats, and on the moors at the summit ling and purple heather, are all the bleak hills can bear. The lower valleys were in old times thickly wooded with shortish trees, and bracken is abundant everywhere. Millstone grit country is always rich in water; scores of rocky streams (becks in West Riding speech) tumble vigorously down from the moorland to the winding valleys below. The grit is fringed with coal and pocketed with iron to the south. Poor farming country, but amply provided with streams and in the old days with sheep, the West Riding thus possessed the wool and water necessary for the manufacture of cloth, and the incentive to weave it offered by the absence of good farming prospects. For centuries wool was spun and cloth woven by hand in upland hamlets or isolated cottages in the folds of the hills. The steep, wooded, rocky valleys were, except at the site of ford or bridge, largely uninhabited; the grey stone houses stood each on its beck just below the brow of the hills. Towards the end of the eighteenth century this world began to be turned upside down; as the textile processes began to be performed increasingly with the aid of water-power, the clothiers were drawn down to the valleys where the rivers were larger and more powerful. In 1812 cropping-frames run by water-power were invented and introduced. The croppers, dreading to be driven from employment by these machines, combined in bands known as Luddites to break the frames on their way to the manufacturers and attack the mills which housed them. The most notable attacks of this kind occurred in 1812, the year of Patrick Brontë's marriage, in a nearby mill within his curacy. The next development in the coming of the Industrial Revolution was the substitution of steam for water-power, and the gradual application of steam-driven machinery to all textile processes. For this development the West Riding, with its handy coal and iron, was admirably equipped, and its progress was rapid.

Thus the Brontës were born at the end of the centuries-old domestic system of cloth manufacture, in a remote upland hamlet the product of that system, which lay not far from the cradle of the Industrial Revolution. By the time they were grown to womanhood the steam age was almost in full swing. The period of their youth was marked in the West Riding by a great and sudden increase in wealth, by the rise, in fact, of the wealthy manufacturing

middle class. It was this social phenomenon which created
the local demand for governesses, for this new class wished
their children to be educated like those of the gentry.

This period was also marked by a great increase in population and by the beginning of railways. The West Riding
does not easily lend itself, however, to transport of any
kind. The interlocking hills and steep narrow valleys obliged the traveller to toil continually up steep slopes,
traverse wild stretches of barren windswept moor, and
descend steep slopes to cross a river and begin the process
of ascent once more. The railway and even the canal have
to tunnel frequently to maintain a reasonable continuity of
level. In the Brontës' youth the railway came as far as
Keighley. There was no conveyance from Haworth to
Keighley save a hired gig and a carrier's cart.

The village of Haworth lies on the slope of a steep hillside, four miles up a winding valley from the town of
Keighley, eight miles over wild steep moorland from the
township of Hebden Bridge, ten miles over high rolling
hills from Bradford, ten over high rolling hills from
Halifax, my own native town. The church, not now the
church the Brontës knew but another on the same site,
stands at the top of a long, steep, narrow paved street. The
houses of Haworth, built (of course) of millstone grit, are
dark in hue but brightly clean as to window-curtains and
doorsteps. Turning to the left through a narrow entry
somewhat like a private backyard, we reach Church Lane,
and passing the church come to the parsonage. The grey
house, two-storeyed, with windows on either side the door,
stands at right angles to the lane, and looks out over a little
oblong garden, across the graveyard crammed with up-

right and horizontal tombstones, to the church, whose tower stands out well against a background of green hills. Behind the parsonage, a little farther along the lane, is the stile to the field footpath which leads to the moors.

To Haworth, then, on a spring day in 1820, came the Brontë family, their household goods climbing the long steep street in seven carts.

Haworth was of immense significance in the three novelists' lives.

Mrs Brontë died of cancer there, and her sister Miss Elizabeth Branwell came from Cornwall to look after her brother-in-law and his family of six. The change from Penzance, with its mild air, bright blue sea, sub-tropical vegetation of palms, abundant flowers and long warm summers, to the rainy, snowy, cold, grey, wind-swept Haworth was not agreeable to Miss Branwell, who always retained a gloomy view of all things Yorkshire. Miss Branwell was a gentlewoman, who brought up her nieces to be admirable housewives, good at their needle, with excellent manners and a strong sense of duty. But she lived much in her bedroom, except when she read the papers to her brother-in-law – which, by the way, she did extremely well – and she was not a mother, or anything like one, to the little Brontës. It is noticeable that in their letters they always call her *Aunt*, never *Auntie* or *Aunt Bessie*, and in all the three hundred or so letters of Charlotte which have been preserved, there is never a single reference to her which could be called affectionate.

By the transport standards of those days Haworth was quite a long way from Bradford where alone Mr Brontë had friends. This remoteness, coupled with his wife's death and his own turn of mind, made him into an unsociable recluse. Whether he was the ferociously stern parent which Mrs Gaskell depicted, whether the Brontës were frightened by his matutinal pistol-shooting and solitary meals, or whether (more probably) they regarded each as just one of Papa's tiresome habits, we cannot know; but it is certain that to the ordinary fearsomeness of the early nineteenth-century parent the Reverend Patrick added some reserve and temper of his own, which Haworth accentuated. Thus the little Brontës lacked both a mother's and a father's tenderness, while subjected in full to the discipline of a family régime. They drew nearer to each other in a defensive alliance, and also devoted themselves to animal pets. This devotion continued throughout their lives, as the many references to Emily's fierce mastiff Keeper, Anne's silky black and white spaniel Flossy, a succession of kittens and occasional canaries, hawks and geese, abundantly testify.

The farther from the moderating influence of town, the more strongly marked are native characteristics. Haworth and its outlying farms and clothiers' homes was 'Yorkshire' to a high degree, and the Brontës' lifelong servant Tabitha Aykroyd (Tabby), who helped to bring up the children and was always admitted to a knowledge of family affairs, was an essentially Yorkshire woman. So was the later housemaid, Martha Brown. Now a type of people less like Celts than the denizens of the West Riding could hardly be imagined. By birth they are of mingled Anglo-Saxon and Danish descent. By nature they are robust, practical, sensible, efficient; strongly suspicious of anything excessive in speech, fond of 'brass', given to a broad rough humour and independent to the point of perversity. Their secret romance, beneath their practical exterior, is this stubborn freedom, this determined independence, this indomitable tenacity of purpose. Thus the combination of Celtic blood and Yorkshire upbringing in the Brontës is a most singular and striking mixture of violently contrasting elements. The mixing in this case was very thorough, for the Brontës felt themselves to be, spoke of themselves as, English, Yorkshire girls, though of course they were not ignorant of their Irish descent.

Haworth lies in the heart of the moors. The impact of the wild moorland on the Brontës, especially on Emily, was not only aesthetic but ethical. 'My sister Emily,' says Charlotte, 'loved the moors.' She 'did not describe as one whose eye and taste alone found pleasure in the prospect; her native hills were far more to her than a spectacle; they were what she lived in, and by . . . she found in the bleak solitude many and dear delights; and not the least and best loved was – liberty.' It was the sense of freedom, of escape from all frustration, the wild exhilaration to be found in battling with wind and weather on those sweeping slopes of livid grass, those sombre and turbulent masses of rock and heather, which nourished the Brontës.

But with the best will in the world one could not call Haworth a centre of culture. The census of 1831 gives the population of Haworth and its dependent hamlets as 5835, but even this small number would be scattered about the neighbouring hills. There were few educated people or gentry among them. Some millowners of the newly risen type before alluded to, who as yet had had little opportunity for education, employed most of the population in

their worsted mills. That the Brontës enjoyed and appreciated the strength of the Yorkshire character is evident in
the Yorkshire portraits in their novels, that the ostentation,
the love of 'brass' of the manufacturers whose children they
taught aroused in them a scornful derision is no less clear.
But the deepest feeling of all except Emily about their
neighbours was that expressed by Jane Eyre when she
speaks of being 'buried with inferior minds'. The terrible
frustration of this burial, the anguish of being shut from the
sun of knowledge into a dark and narrow grave, the pain
of struggling to free oneself from the living impediments
without hurting the feelings of those who compose them –
this was the feeling which Haworth inflicted upon the
Brontës, especially Charlotte and Branwell.

All these factors, which made the Brontës at one and the
same time passionately devoted natives and strangers in a
strange land, brought them a terrible loneliness, but saved
them from that provincialism which accepts the scene, the
people, the manners and customs of one's own neighbourhood as of supreme merit and universal sanction. Aunt's
reminiscences of Cornwall, Papa's of Ireland, the fibre of
their own minds and hearts, reminded them that Yorkshire,
dearly though they loved it, was not the whole world. Thus
a certain measure of detachment was theirs; they were able
to lift their heads and observe objectively what was around
them.

DAYDREAM

Their loneliness had another, a supremely important,
result.

> 'We wove a web in childhood,
> A web of sunny air,'

wrote Charlotte in 1835. It is only recently that, by protracted research, the true and terrible significance of these
lines has been fully revealed. After the death of Maria and
Elizabeth in 1825, the four remaining Brontës became
dreamers, and recorders in writing, of shared daydreams.

All children love to play at being grown-up, and it is
perhaps from this instinctive educational process that their
habit of make-believe springs. When they are lonely or
unhappy, make-believe offers a way of escape from an un-
satisfying into a satisfying world. The make-believe thus
develops into daydream, that is into wish-fulfilment fantasy, where the characters, types of the child's unconscious
desires and fears, experience adventures in which the child's
will always prevails, even if a distortion of real physical
laws is necessary to accomplish it. Children who have a
storytelling bent, those who when grown will become the
novelists and dramatists of their generation, are apt to
weave these daydreams into story cycles, sagas, from which
when alone they select episodes at will for mental re-
enactment. References to this practice of daydream may be
found in the fictions of such diverse novelists as George
Eliot (*Mill on the Floss*), Du Maurier (*Peter Ibbetson*),
Kipling (*Brushwood Boy*) and Barrie (*Sentimental Tommy*),
while the existence of Hartley Coleridge's imaginary kingdom, Ejuxria, is recorded by his brother (*Memoir*), to
whom he often recounted its affairs.

The Brontë children did not differ, then, from other
lonely and imaginative children when they constructed

daydream worlds. What distinguishes their case is first that
they shared their dream-world in common. In early years
all four shaped one world together, later two worlds were
shared in pairs. Their second difference from other day-
dreaming children is that they put their dream-worlds into
writing. The tiny booklets, often less than two inches
square, with their minute Brontë hand-printing (to read
which a magnifying-glass is necessary), for long the
wonder and mystery of all Brontë students, have been
coaxed, through the careful transcriptions of earlier editors
and finally through the interpretative analysis of Fannie
Elizabeth Ratchford, librarian of the University of Texas,
to reveal their secret. One hundred of the booklets, equal in
wordage to the total published works of the three Brontë
sisters, have been traced and studied; the whole mass
has proved to be a saga of the Brontës' imaginary
world.

By a stroke of immense good fortune we know exactly
how this world originated. Charlotte writes:

Our plays were established: *Young Men*, June 1826; *Our
Fellows*, July 1827; *Islanders*, December 1827 ... The *Young
Men's* play took its rise from some wooden soldiers Branwell
had; *Our Fellows* from Aesop's Fables; and the *Islanders* from
several events which happened. I will sketch out the origin of
our plays more explicitly if I can. First: *Young Men*. Papa
bought Branwell some wooden soldiers at Leeds; when Papa
came home it was night, and we were in bed, so next morning
Branwell came to our door with a box of soldiers. Emily and I
jumped out of bed, and I snatched up one and exclaimed,
'This is the Duke of Wellington! This shall be the Duke!'
When I had said this Emily likewise took one up and said it

should be hers; when Anne came down she said one should
be hers ... – *History of the Year 1829*

Branwell in his *History of the Young Men* (1836) con-
firms this story of the box of a dozen soldiers brought from
Leeds, adding:

> These were the 12s ... what is contained in this history is a
> statement of what Myself, Charlotte, Emily and Anne really
> pretended did happen among the 'Young Men' (that being the
> name we gave them) during the period of nearly six years.

He goes on to tell how the Twelves (i.e. the twelve
wooden soldiers animated into young men) founded a
kingdom on the African coast, elected Charlotte's beloved
Duke of Wellington as king and built a city which they
called Great Glass Town. The Twelves were helped in
their work by four Chief Genii named Tallii, Brannii,
Emmii and Annii, that is, Charlotte, Branwell, Emily and
Anne. Later, various members of the Twelves founded
allied kingdoms, each with a Glass Town capital.

Thus arose the Glass Town confederacy; a whole world,
with newspapers and magazines, pictures and politics, poets
and historians, publishers and booksellers, actresses and
generals, of its own. Charlotte conducts the romances of
the characters, Branwell the battles and parliamentary
struggles. They bring out many numbers of *Young Men's
Magazine*, written in their tiny script on tiny sheets of
paper, stitched together in grey or brown or blue covers
made of sugar-wrappers. In these magazines are poems,
character sketches of prominent persons, essays, stories,

histories, reviews of new books, accounts of the latest paintings, even advertisements. All are written by the Brontës in the character of Glass Town personalities – for example, Young Soult, the famous Glass Town poet, is a pseudonym of Branwell's; all refer to Glass Town happenings, Glass Town persons, Glass Town scenery, Glass Town scandals. The pictures referred to were Glass Town landscapes and Glass Town portraits, painted by Charlotte and Branwell as Glass Town artists.

In 1831 Charlotte went away to school. The four Chief Genii in solemn conference decided to destroy Great Glass Town, and the teeming city was forthwith wiped out – an event which Charlotte records in a romantic poem (*The Trumpet Hath Sounded*, 1831). This doom was soon retracted and Glass Town stories resumed, but it seems that during Charlotte's absence Emily and Anne broke away from the Glass Town dream-world and invented another of their own. There are certain important differences between this world of Emily's, Gondal, and the world of Charlotte and Branwell, especially the new Angrian wing which the elder Brontës now proceeded to add.

Angria, a kingdom lying to the east of Great Glass Town, was conquered by two Angrian characters, the Dukes of Zamorna and Northangerland. These two Dukes, opponents always, were both dark, ruthless, fascinating Byronic hero-villains. Both were irresistible to women. Their marriages and illicit amours are the themes of many a poem and tale of Charlotte's, while their political struggles in the Angrian parliament and their battlefields are Branwell's inspiration. Certain distortions of reality – the power of resurrection, a disregard of time and space, a severance of cause and effect, are carried over into Angria from the childish Glass Town. Angria is a place of marble columns and rich draperies, of majestic mountains and stately rivers, of women dying for love and men always scornful, handsome and magniloquent. In a word it is an escape world; a world where actions which excited Charlotte's severest censure in real life were not merely condoned but enjoyed. There could be no clearer case of wish-fulfilment daydreams, the indulging of desires which in real life were never allowed to pass Charlotte's mental censor.

Gondal on the other hand is a northern land, a land of mist and moor and wild winds, and as far as can be judged from the scantier materials available, a land of stern inexorable logic. The Queen of Gondal was a great woman of great and not always lawful passions, but her actions produced the consequences which they would produce in the real world; evil produced evil, and good good, in Emily's Gondal, and the lot of the inhabitants was a realistic mingling of both.

In these imaginary worlds the young Brontës spent a great deal of their time. When Emily was 'brushing the carpet' or Anne sewing or Charlotte learning to iron, or Emily and Anne walking home from Keighley, their minds were far away; outwardly demure, reserved, well-behaved, Christian, inwardly they were conquering kingdoms, assisting at Councils of State, wielding arrogant power or tenderest love, and planning the stories, essays and poems in which they recorded these experiences.

Besides their extraordinary intrinsic value as a psychological study and a revelation of genius in infancy, the

Angrian and Gondal documents have a very great importance in the study of the Brontës' works.

To begin with, they reveal the inferiority of the unhappy
Branwell. Charlotte in her Angrian writings often pokes
fun at the bad verse, tedious prose and affected mannerisms
of 'Young Soult', and the specimens reveal that her criticisms are only too well-founded. It is clear, too, that
Branwell had no hand in *Wuthering Heights*. Charlotte and
Branwell shared a dream-world, talked of it, corresponded
about it, till 1839 at least; Emily and Branwell parted
dream-company eight years earlier. The story of *Wuthering
Heights* is adumbrated in a Gondal poem; Branwell never
contributed to Gondal.

The difference in ethic between Angria and Gondal
illuminates the difference between Charlotte and Emily
which appears in their poems and novels. One cannot avoid
a feeling of discomfort on reading some passages in
Charlotte's published works immediately after some of her
Angrian stories, for in her published works Charlotte
strongly condemns what in Angria she loves. Jane Eyre
will not become Rochester's mistress, Lucy Snowe despises
bright silks for wear; but in Angria illicit love is glorified
and the wives of Zamorna and Northangerland are clad
with a richness suitable to their station. Emily has no such
dual standard; she does not condemn the Gondal Queen
Augusta or the *Wuthering Heights* Heathcliff for a nature
they cannot help, but neither does she justify their op-
pressive actions.

It is clear that the daydream-script habit was an essential
part of the Brontë mentality and exerted a strongly forma-
tive influence on their work. Clear prototypes of Rochester

and some *Villette* characters exist in Angria and even some of the actual incidents of Charlotte's novels are to be found there, while many of the best-known Brontë poems belong to the Angrian or Gondal cycle. Again, the mere writing of these thousands upon thousands of words, the mere experimenting in so many diverse metres, the mere drawing of so many different characters, gave the Brontës an amount of literary practice which made them experienced writers before they began to compose a line with a view to publication. The small physical space into which this writing was crammed and the tiny delicate print of which it consisted, too, undoubtedly influenced the Brontës' composition. When one is printing tiny letters on a tiny sheet one thinks quite a while before one writes, for a wrong word means an erasure or correction, very uncomfortable in such cramped quarters. The Brontës' fine English depends very largely on their admirable choice of words. Their day-dream scripts gave them a long and strict training in word-selection.

For the Brontës as human beings, as opposed to the Brontës as writers, their long preoccupation with these 'worlds below' was less happy. Their daydreams had grave psychological dangers. Charlotte in a letter writes of 'the fiery imagination that at times eats me up and makes me feel society, as it is, wretchedly insipid'. Indulgence in day-dream unfits the dreamer for the ordinary social relations of friendship, love and marriage, for all real people and situations seem 'wretchedly insipid' and disappointing compared with their wish-fulfilment versions. The dreamer has, too, a refuge from all real trials and troubles to which he increasingly resorts. Increasingly he shirks real life, till

at last if he be forced to abandon his dream, like the
Lady of Shalott he perishes beneath the fearful impact
of reality.

Branwell, we feel, perished spiritually thus, unable to
cope with stern reality after fantasy delights. His sisters
were saved partly by Charlotte's passion for culture, which
helped to occupy their minds, partly by their own strength
and genius. Charlotte deliberately wrote a farewell to
Angria in 1839. Emily, as her poems show, equally deliberately declined to sacrifice the kingdom of her imagination.
But the step from Haworth to Gondal was a step from the
real to the fictitious only, not to the fantastic; the danger
for her was far less serious. Anne's fervid piety probably
restrained indulgence of any kind within moderate limits.
But what a terrible expenditure of energy these dream-
worlds involved! Would the Brontës have died so young
if they had not so exhausted themselves?

EDUCATIONAL

The receiving and giving of education provided the
medium for the prime external experiences of the Brontës;
education was the point at which they touched normal life.

In childhood, while they sadly lacked human com-
panionship, they were not without printed food for their
minds. The family saw five newspapers of differing political
complexions each week; the children read and discussed
them eagerly, encouraged by their father. Mrs Gaskell has
recorded, too, the presence of many standard works of a
solid kind up and down the Parsonage; the best-bound in
Mr Brontë's study, the tattered – for the money did not

stretch to re-binding – on bedroom shelves. The children belonged, later, to a circulating library in Keighley. Besides direct evidence, the whole structure of Angria shows that the little Brontës were avid readers. One cannot imitate without models, and all departments of Angrian affairs – art, history, literature, geography, politics – mimic their real prototypes closely.

Unluckily for Branwell, he scarcely experienced the normal contacts which school life supplies. He was educated almost entirely at home by his father, studying prescribed hours each day. Mr Brontë, whom home study had brought from Emdale to Cambridge, no doubt envisaged a similar career for his brilliant son. He forgot how much time he had to spend on parish affairs; he forgot that boys need playmates; he probably was ignorant of the weakness and volatility of his son's nature; he certainly knew nothing of Angria. Branwell, with no domestic tasks to tie him, continually left free, bored and lonely for hours on end, sought company in Haworth village, where he was often asked to brighten festive occasions with his admired eloquence. A drink or two, he found, made his tongue flow faster. Presently the landlord of the Black Bull knew him well, and sometimes sent for the precocious lad to come and amuse a chance guest and help him out with his bottle – it was only a step; the Black Bull stands at the top of the steep Haworth hill, a stone's throw from the Parsonage.

The girls were more fortunate. After the abortive Cowan Bridge experiment in 1825, they were taught by their aunt for the next six years, but in 1831 Charlotte, now fifteen, was sent to board at the Woolers' school at Roe Head, a pleasant roomy country house lying not far from her father's earlier curacy at Hartshead, and in the very heart of the former Luddite country.

Miss Margaret Wooler, the head of the school, was a good simple culture-loving woman, for whom Charlotte had a lasting love and respect; she perceived and encouraged Charlotte's scholastic ability. The little school held only some ten pupils, but two of these became Charlotte's life-long friends. Charlotte Brontë, Ellen Nussey and Mary Taylor always occupied the first three places in class order; sometimes the places moved round amongst these three, but they were never invaded from below. Ellen and Mary, who lived in neighbouring West Riding townships, were interestingly different in character and upbringing. Ellen's family was Tory and Church of England; one of her brothers was a clergyman who became a missionary; an uncle had been a Court physician; she herself was calm, sensible, fair-complexioned and religious in a decorous and lady-like style. In later life she was apt to make with her needle old-maidish little gifts for her friends at which Mary Taylor laughed, their purpose being obscure. The Taylors were Radical and Nonconformist textile manufacturers, independent, impetuous, argumentative and unconventional; Mary was strongly feminist in thought and speech. Charlotte stayed as guest in both Ellen's and Mary's homes in years to come, and they visited her in Haworth; then presently Mary Taylor emigrated to New Zealand, and kept in touch with Charlotte only by rare letters. Ellen remained in the West Riding, unmarried; Charlotte's many letters to her and Ellen's own descriptions are our best source of information about the external circumstances of the Brontës.

From Roe Head Charlotte brought two friendships, the idea of gaining her living by teaching, and the germ of *Shirley*. After three half-years there, having learned all the Miss Woolers had to teach her, she withdrew to Haworth to pass on her instruction to her sisters.

In 1835 Miss Wooler invited Charlotte to teach where she had been taught. Part of the bargain was that one of her sisters should have the advantages of education at the school, and Emily accompanied her to Roe Head. But Emily could not endure the sensation of imprisonment inevitable in even the mildest school. Homesickness, longing for the moors and liberty to roam them swept down on her every morning and pierced her heart with anguish; from a sense of duty she struggled valiantly to command herself; the conflict, silent but fierce, almost broke her health. After three months she was recalled to Haworth at Charlotte's instance, and the mild, pensive, docile and pious Anne took her place. Next year Emily again attempted school, this time as a teacher in a school of forty girls at Law Hill near Halifax; she sustained the fearful struggle with her own nature for six months before yielding and returning home. Meanwhile Anne's health gave cause for anxiety to Charlotte, who thought Miss Wooler unsympathetic on the subject; the school had been moved to a less agreeable site, Charlotte herself was almost overpowered by depression, and after a tiff with Miss Wooler (soon forgiven) the two girls returned to Haworth. It must be remembered that in addition to the ordinary miseries of homesickness and loss of liberty, the Brontës when they were parted felt in some measure cut off from their imaginary worlds.

The six years from 1835 to 1841 were a period of honest but heartbreaking struggle, during which all four Brontës strove manfully to conquer their own nature and fit into conventional wage-earning niches in the outer world, in vain. After the Roe Head experience Charlotte twice, and Anne twice, became governesses in private families; the experience they gained in agony later gave masterpieces to the world. Branwell, whose gift in painting was thought to deserve tuition at the Royal Academy school, was perhaps by his own fault disappointed of this plan. An Angrian narrative, *Charles Wentworth's visit to Verdopolis*, written by Branwell two months after his visit to London, might give us the whole story of the failure if it had but survived in full. Wentworth's 'instinctive fear of ending his pleasure by approaching reality', which keeps him from entering the great buildings of the metropolis or presenting his letters of introduction, the 'little squibs of rums' with which he strives to overcome his depression, are only too probably reminiscences of Branwell's own behaviour in London. At any rate, from this time onward the boy descends into the abyss. His attempt to set up as a portrait painter in Bradford failed. He acted as tutor for six months in Furness, then – alas, poor brilliant Branwell! – became a railway booking clerk, first at one and then the other of two tiny stations near Halifax, where by his own account 'malignant yet cold debauchery . . . too often marked my conduct'. By this the poor boy means only that he drank to excess sometimes and got a few pounds into debt; his tendency to self-dramatization, always marked, went to disastrous lengths a few years later. He lost every post after a few months.

The only happiness of this period came to the Brontës

through their father's first curate (paid for with the help of the Pastoral Aid Society), the Rev William Weightman, a 'bonny, pleasant, light-hearted, good-tempered, generous, careless,' friendly young man, a flirt as handsome young men often are, a good speaker and a good classical scholar. 'Celia Amelia', as they called him, came to tea with the Brontës as well as with all the other girls in the neighbourhood; he talked intelligently, he sent them valentines; he arranged for them to be invited to Keighley to hear him lecture. (They reached Haworth with two clerical escorts at midnight; there was not enough coffee to go round, and Aunt was cross.) Charlotte painted his portrait and liked him; even Emily liked him; Anne loved him. Weightman is the single bright gleam, the only piece of normal care-free young happiness, in the Brontës' lives.

The gleam was brief, but perhaps stimulating, for it was during the Weightman period that the Brontës conceived their great project. They had proved that governessing away from home made them wretched, but teaching was the only gainful occupation open to spinster ladies in those days; why then not start a school of their own? Aunt Branwell astonishingly offered to lend them £100 for the project; Miss Wooler might yield up to them her school. At this point, 'friends', says Charlotte, recommended her to delay beginning the school for six months, and spend the intervening time in some school on the Continent, learning French. Schools in England were so numerous, competition so great, that some such step towards attaining superiority was essential to success, and so on. So Charlotte wrote to her aunt; but the impulse towards Brussels was really initiated by letters from Martha and Mary Taylor, who, at school in Brussels, were touring Europe on holiday with their brother. Of these she wrote to Ellen Nussey:

> I hardly know what swelled to my throat as I read her letter ... such an urgent thirst to see – to know – to learn ... I was tantalized by the consciousness of faculties unexercised ... I so longed to become something better than I am ...
>
> – Letter of 7 August 1841

Thus the great adventure of Charlotte's life took shape. Aunt agreed to lend the extra money required, and in 1842 Mr Brontë escorted Charlotte and Emily to the *Maison d'Education pour les jeunes demoiselles* conducted by M. and Madame Heger, in the Rue d'Isabelle, Brussels, an establishment containing some fifty pupils and three or four teachers.

In spite of the difficulties offered by strange language, manners and religion, the Brontës made such admirable progress as pupils that they drew upon themselves the special attention of Professor Heger. This time Emily's will-power triumphed; she endured exile and constraint with fortitude, impressing M. Heger as having the finer mind of the two, a mind 'like a man's' in scope and power. The two girls remained at the Pensionnat Heger until November 1842. In early October the lively William Weightman died; in late October Aunt Branwell died; as soon as they heard this latter news the Brontës started for home. The Hegers then wrote to Mr Brontë proposing that the girls, or at least one of them, should return to the Pensionnat as a pupil-teacher, and thus complete their interrupted studies while enjoying a 'sweet independence'. As

Anne and Branwell were both away, being governess and tutor in the Robinson family at Thorp Green, at least one of the girls was needed at home. Emily remained in Haworth; Charlotte returned to Brussels alone in January 1843 and remained there for a year.

This is the external story of the Brontës' Brussels adventure; this is how it appeared to Mr Brontë in 1844. How it appeared to Charlotte is a different matter. The present writer believes that Charlotte loved Constantin Heger. She found in this irascible, fiery, exacting little professor, with his high integrity and passion for letters, the first satisfying real example of the 'master' type, which she had portrayed many times, with obvious sexual admiration and desire, in the Angrian world. This 'master' type is the typical spinster's hero; he expresses the unconscious yearning of the unsought woman – or the unsatisfactorily sought; Charlotte had rejected proposals from stiff Henry Nussey and an impulsive curate – because to be sought by a man so powerful that he despises the world which has despised her is her greatest possible sexual triumph. Professor Heger was not merely the master by character and masculinity, but in mind and intellectual acquirements. She could rest on a strength which she genuinely trusted and admired. And he was real; warmly, exasperatingly, affectionately real – and he liked and admired and scolded Mees Charlotte. All her strong starved nature turned to him and bloomed beneath his interest. The evidence is all in favour of this love – for example: Mme Heger's growing reserve, of which Charlotte fancies she begins 'to perceive the reason . . . it sometimes makes me laugh, and at other times nearly cry'; the incident when, left alone during the long summer holiday,

Charlotte entered a Catholic cathedral and made 'a real confession' to a priest; her comment later to Ellen, that she returned to Brussels 'against my conscience, prompted by what then seemed an irresistible impulse. I was punished for my selfish folly by a total withdrawal for more than two years of happiness and peace of mind.' If these do not convince, her letters to M. Heger will surely do so, especially those passages lamenting the lack of reply.

> When day by day I await a letter, and when day by day disappointment comes . . . I lose appetite and sleep – I pine away.
> – Translated from Letter, 24 July 1844

> I strove to restrain my tears, to utter no complaint . . . Day and night I find neither rest nor peace. If I sleep I am disturbed by tormenting dreams in which I see you always severe, always grave, always incensed against me . . . If my master withdraws his friendship from me entirely I shall be altogether without hope . . . – Translated from Letter, 8 January 1845

If this, from a young woman of twenty-eight to a man, be not the language of love, it is difficult to surmise in what that language consists. Mme Heger evidently thought it such, for Constantin presently desired Charlotte to write to him at the boys' school next to the Pensionnat Heger where he acted as professor, since his wife disliked his receiving her letters. That it was conscious love on Charlotte's part is a different matter – indeed clearly it was not, for she declined indignantly to conduct any such clandestine correspondence.

Charlotte returned to Haworth in January 1844 partly because of her growing misery in Brussels, partly because of growing misery at home. Mr Brontë's sight was failing, and the protracted wretchedness of waiting for a cataract operation was upon him; Branwell was frightening Anne by his odd behaviour at Thorp Green. After the bustle of the Pensionnat, Haworth seemed deadly quiet. Charlotte pushed forward bravely with the Brontë school project, printing circulars and distributing them through her Wooler and Nussey and Taylor friends, but the situation of Haworth was too retired, the teachers too unknown, to tempt; not a single pupil offered herself.

In the summer of 1845 a crushing blow fell on the family through Branwell, who received a note of stern dismissal from his employer, the Reverend Mr Robinson. The unhappy lad had perhaps been silly enough to attempt love-passages with Mrs Robinson, who he fancied returned his passion. How much, or whether at all, she had really encouraged him will never now be known, but Branwell in the anguish of his disappointment exaggerated the affair into a regular intrigue, horrifying his father and his sisters. (To Charlotte this travesty of her own by now sternly repressed passion must have been particularly nauseating.) For the next three years Branwell gave himself increasingly to brandy and opium; he declined all work; nights through which he kept his poor old father awake by his drunken raving, days occupied in devices to get hold of the money to buy a dram, became commonplaces at the Parsonage. Though Aunt Branwell's little legacies were now available to finance a school, the scheme was perforce abandoned.

Emily and Anne could still find solace in Gondal, but Charlotte felt as though they were all buried alive in Haworth. Their attempts to secure a life of more variety, more action, more communication with their fellow-men, through their ability as teachers, had failed; a harsh fate thrust them ruthlessly back into the narrow and restricted sphere from which they had so earnestly struggled to escape. At night when, father and brother retired to bed and Branwell settled to a drunken sleep at last, the girls paced round the parlour table as was their custom, arms interlaced around each other's waists, their musings must have been sad indeed. Anne was twenty-five, Emily twenty-seven, Charlotte nearly thirty, and they had done nothing, nothing!

LITERARY CAREER

When hemmed in on one side or another by dark walls of misery and frustration, active and courageous spirits will struggle for other avenues of expression. In the autumn of 1845 Charlotte accidentally lighted upon a manuscript volume of verse in Emily's handwriting. Of late the girls had not shown each other their writings; these poems were new to Charlotte and she was struck, as well she might be, by their wild power. At once the idea of publication seized her. Emily was fiercely angry at Charlotte's unlicensed intrusion into her notebook and her mind; it took hours, says Charlotte, to reconcile her to her sister's discovery, days to persuade her that her poems merited publication. While the struggle raged, Anne mildly produced a selection of verse pieces from her own pen. Eventually an attempt to publish a volume of poems by all three sisters was decided.

They had no idea how one achieved such a publication, but by dint of writing round to various publishers Charlotte at last discovered how to proceed. In January 1846 we find her writing to Messrs Aylott & Jones of Paternoster Row to inquire whether they would undertake the publication of an octavo volume of poems, either at their own risk or on the authors' account. Mr Aylott evidently replied promptly and favourably, for three days later Charlotte is writing to him again about the format of the volume. She bought a book on printing to be able to discuss type and size of page, and her whole correspondence with the firm is a charming compound of innocence and businesslike lucidity. The Brontës paid £31 10s (ten guineas each) for the publication of a single volume of poems. They spent £2 on advertisement at first, to which £10 was added later. The journals to which review copies were to be sent were carefully specified. The sisters chose the neutral pen-names of Currer, Ellis and Acton Bell, not wishing to expose themselves to the prejudice or the condescension then often displayed by critics towards women writers, but scrupling to take names positively masculine. ('Currer', by the way, was an Angrian name.)

We do not know exactly when the novels *The Professor*, *Wuthering Heights* and *Agnes Grey* were begun, but it was most probably immediately after the stimulus of Mr Aylott's first favourable reply, for in April Charlotte asks whether he would be willing to publish three one-volume tales, then in course of preparation by the Bells. Mr Aylott, a strictly pious gentleman, shocked by the suggestion of publishing fiction, declined the project, but offered advice. The tales were then 'perseveringly obtruded upon various publishers' for more than a year, receiving each time an 'ignominious and abrupt' dismissal.

The repeated exposure of one's cherished work thus to rejection is an extremely trying experience for sensitive young people; there are indeed whole lifetimes which do not yield sharper or more abundant sensations than this cycle of hope, suspense and cruel disappointment. Meanwhile, in July the poems appeared – and fell to the ground practically unheeded. A review or two here and there praised Ellis's 'evident power of wing', but of the carefully prepared edition there were sold only two copies. The Brontë sisters consumed their disappointment privately. No word of their literary hopes must reach poor Branwell, no additional worry must be heaped upon poor Papa. They continued staunchly, bravely, perseveringly, secretly, to obtrude their novels upon publishers. In August, Charlotte accompanied Mr Brontë to Manchester for the cataract operation; it was necessary to stay in lodgings for five weeks there, with a nurse to attend him. On the very day of the operation *The Professor* was returned to her hands once again. She dispatched it to yet another publisher – and began to write *Jane Eyre*.

Some time in the first half of 1847 *Wuthering Heights* and *Agnes Grey* were accepted by the publisher Newby, apparently on condition of some money payment by the authors, and were in proof by August. *The Professor*, however, was still rejected, until in July Charlotte sent it to the sixth she had tried, the reputable firm of Messrs Smith, Elder. They too refused it, but in terms so rational, so discriminating, that for the first time its author felt encouraged. She was just completing *Jane Eyre*, which was of the three-volume length then considered proper. Before the end of August she sent the new book to them, still under the pseudonym of Currer Bell. Their reader, W. S. Williams, expressed such enthusiasm for the work that George Smith laughed – till he read it himself. It was published in October and achieved a resounding success, receiving the immediate praise of such men as Leigh Hunt, George Henry Lewes and, above all, Thackeray, to whom Charlotte gratefully dedicated the second edition, brought out in January 1848. There were, of course, adverse comments, but on the whole the reviews which poured in were long and favourable, the book sold well (Charlotte received five hundred pounds for the copyright) and was pronounced decidedly the best novel of the season. The correspondence with Williams began which, as Charlotte said, brought life and light to the torpid retirement where they lived like dormice, and now at last she ventured to tell the secret to her father.

Meanwhile, in December 1847, *Wuthering Heights* and *Agnes Grey* appeared. Only 250 copies were printed; the format was not as agreeable as that of *Jane Eyre*, and errors corrected in the proofs had been allowed to remain in the text. The novels were ill received – so was *The Tenant of Wildfell Hall*, published the following summer – and what was worse, they were attributed to the same hand as penned *Jane Eyre*. The obviously pseudonymous nature of the names Currer, Ellis and Acton Bell gave scope to all kinds of speculations: the Bells were supposed to be one person and the later novels crude, early or later rejected productions of the author of *Jane Eyre*, or they were three persons of different sex, the sexes arranged in varying proportions amongst the three. The vexation reached its height in July 1848 when the American publishers of *Jane Eyre*, who had signed a contract for Currer Bell's next novel, found another American publisher announcing a brace of new novels from Currer Bell's hand – the iniquitous Newby having sold the sheets of *Wuthering Heights* and *Agnes Grey* under these false pretences. The American publishers complained to Smith, Elder and the complaint was passed to Haworth. Horrified by the accusation of double-dealing to which their mild little mystery had exposed them, the sisters decided that they must confront Smith, Elder personally at once. Charlotte and Anne hurried through their household duties, sent off a box by a cart, walked to Keighley through a storm, caught the night mail, were whisked off to London and entered the publishing house of Smith, Elder in Cornhill early the following morning.

The arrival of the two small, shy, oddly dressed ladies in this bustling establishment, their eventual entrance upon the tall young man who was George Smith and the thunderclap of Charlotte's hurried announcement of her name and 'We are three sisters', while putting into his hand his own letter to Currer Bell, form one of those romantic and delightful episodes of literary history where everything happens just as it should. And what a weekend they passed in London! The opera that night with the handsome Smith and his elegant sisters, church with Williams and his family next morning, dinner at the Smiths' in Bayswater that night, the Academy and National Gallery on Monday and tea at the Williams'; home on Tuesday laden with presents of books. The excitement – and perhaps the reaction of the return to Haworth afterwards – exhausted Charlotte, for whom, if only she would have admitted it, this contact with literary society must surely have been a fulfilment of her dreams. She does not mention Anne's fatigue; perhaps Anne, with less ambition, took London more calmly.

In the months following the publication of *Jane Eyre*, Williams had naturally pressed Charlotte to begin another novel. At first she experienced some anxiety on this subject; her materials, her experience of life, she knew to be slender; her proposal to expand and amend *The Professor* was rejected; yet she was fully determined to write only of what she knew. But this difficulty was now past, for she had begun *Shirley* while an expanding horizon was offering additional materials for future work; Emily and Anne, as far as she could see, were not unduly daunted by the hostile criticisms on their work but prepared to try again; the Bell muddle was cleared up; a genuinely friendly and candid relation had been established between herself and her publishers, who had secured the unused sheets of the *Poems* with a view to second publication, had a contract for Charlotte's next novel, and were ready to take an interest in the other Brontës' future work. It really seemed as if, after the long cold winter of their lives hitherto, a warm and fragrant spring might visit Haworth Parsonage. But it was not to be.

SORROW

Branwell's health was growing rapidly worse. By July 1848 Charlotte reports to Ellen Nussey that his constitution seems shattered. For all that, neither the doctors nor the Brontës thought him so near his end as he actually proved to be; two days before his death he was about as usual in Haworth village. He died, aged thirty-one, after a twenty minutes' struggle on the morning of Sunday, 24 September 1848; tradition says that he had determined to die standing, and when the last agony approached forced himself upright.

By the outside world the death of Branwell could only be regarded as a release for his sisters; but the Brontës were of too noble a nature to view it in that light. As they gazed on the features made handsome again by the marble chill of death, they forgave all his vices, remembered only his early promise, his bright young affection and his woes. Poor Mr Brontë's first grief was anguished, but on the whole he and Anne stood the storm well; Charlotte was laid low with a sharp but short attack of gastritis; Emily unfortunately contracted a cough and cold.

In fact the Sunday after Branwell's death was the last time Emily went out of doors, and she died of consumption on 19 December of that year. The swift course of her illness was made doubly terrible to her sisters by her awful fortitude; she declined to see a doctor or take medicine, and forced herself to continue her ordinary household tasks until muscular strength actually failed her. Expressions of sympathy, offers of help, brought an angry frown; Charlotte and Anne were obliged to sit and listen without stirring to her gasping breath as she tried to feed the dogs or climb the stairs, obliged to watch in silence the swift emaciation of her tall frame. Charlotte obtained a medical opinion on her case through Williams, sending a London physician a description of her symptoms, but it was useless. There came a day when the lingering spray of heather (in bloom) which Charlotte had found after long search in the sheltered crevices of the wintry moors to bring to her sister went unrecognized by Emily's 'dim and indifferent' eyes.

Emily not recognize heather! She must be ill indeed. One noon she suddenly whispered hoarsely to Charlotte: 'If you will send for a doctor, I will see him now.' Even then she declined to retire to bed, but died two hours later on the parlour sofa.

Hardly was she buried when her family perceived that Anne's health too gave cause for alarm. (At this moment of anguish the notorious *Quarterly Review* article on *Vanity Fair* and *Jane Eyre*, saying that Currer Bell, if a woman, must be one who had 'forfeited the society of her sex', came to refuse Charlotte even the escape of pleasurable thoughts of her literary career.) Where Emily showed stern fortitude, Anne showed mild patience; she submitted to doctors' attendance, took all precautions, drank the hated cod-liver oil. But by February Charlotte was using the ominous phrase 'in case she should ever be well enough to go out again'. Towards the end of her life poor gentle Anne conceived a passionate desire to go to Scarborough, which she had visited while in one of her governess situations. In great fear but not liking to refuse what she felt to be a dying wish, Charlotte, accompanied by Ellen Nussey, took her sister to Scarborough in May 1849. Anne looked with quiet love on castle and cliff and sea, drove a donkey mildly on the sands, saw a glorious sunset and died next morning, four days after leaving home.

The Brontës' Irish ancestry no doubt gave them a predisposition to tuberculosis, but we may well inquire why at this particular moment the disease should gallop them thus headlong into the grave. There were, of course, physical reasons. Branwell died of the effects on his lungs of chronic drink and drugs, and as the long years of agony he had caused his sisters closed thus, no doubt they experienced a serious reaction, almost a collapse, after the strain. Emily perhaps caught cold at Branwell's funeral. The situation of the Parsonage, with all those graves clustering round, was unhealthy; the wild winds and driving rain of bleak Haworth made a climate unfavourable to their disease. The girls lived in close quarters, sharing bedrooms and always together; modern precautions against infection were unknown. But when all that has been said, one cannot but feel that these two deaths within six months, of young women thirty and twenty-nine respectively (i.e. past the most dangerous tubercular age), must have had some striking psychological cause. Anne and Emily were inseparable friends in life; it was not altogether surprising that the milder and weaker and younger girl, who had always been delicate, should make haste to follow the stronger of the pair to the grave. But what of Emily's swift decline? Of earlier ill-health on her part we have heard little – though it is true that Emily would not be given to complain.

In family life, even when there is genuine affection between brothers and sisters, the domination of the elders is often felt by the younger to be tiresome. Sometimes this leads to open revolt on the part of the younger, sometimes to secret reserve, sometimes to both. Especially is this the case when the views of life, the ideals, held by younger and elder differ. This situation may have existed in the Brontë family. Emily cannot have been at ease with Miss Branwell's small genteel nature. Charlotte's passionate protective care for her younger sisters perhaps irked Emily's free spirit. There is a disconcerting dialect poem in Charlotte's Glass Town story, *The Foundling*, about a character called

'Eamala' (Yorkshire for Emily) who 'aat of her pocket a knife did pull'.

> And wi' that knoife shoo'd a cutt her throit
> If I hadn't gean her a strait waist-coit;
>   Then shoo flang and jumped
>   And girned and grumped,
> But I didn't caare for her a doit.

Is this a rendering of a real incident in Emily's childhood? An open revolt, unsuccessful and so followed by withdrawal to reserve? Charlotte's enthusiasms were not Emily's. Emily's so much deeper, so much more adult mind perhaps put school in its proper place, disliked the harshness of Charlotte's censorious comment on her neighbours, and viewed Charlotte's ambitions as a mere worldly – and therefore despicable – desire to 'get on'. Charlotte tells us that Emily would fail to defend her most manifest rights, to consult her most legitimate advantage. Emily perhaps regarded such defence as self-seeking and ignoble. In a word, Charlotte thought that Emily always needed an interpreter to stand between her and the world. Did Emily feel that that interpreter could never be Charlotte – feel it but, scorning to defend her rights by wounding others, never say it?

If it were so, it would cohere with Emily's character as it is known to us. Emily loved the wild free moors, Emily loved to be alone, Emily kept the secret places of Gondal alive even when urged to abandon them. Emily was angry when Charlotte read her poems, furious when Charlotte revealed the identity of Ellis Bell to Smith and Williams.

Ellis Bell was not a mere Brontë, but a wild free spirit. Unconsciously Emily always resisted – not with weak petulance but with the serene simplicity of the strong – the invasion of personality with which for affection's sake she was always threatened.

But if it were so, what agony for Emily to have *Wuthering Heights* attributed to Charlotte! The constant praise of Charlotte's work above her own, with its different values which Emily repudiated, the savage and completely uncomprehending reviews of *Wuthering Heights* which called Ellis Bell 'dogged, brutal and morose', were painful enough; Mrs Gaskell records how Charlotte's pleasure over *Jane Eyre* was ruined by seeing Emily's resolute endurance of her terrible pangs of disappointment over these reviews. But to have the last recess of her mind, her novel, the product of her own special peculiar self handed over to this elder sister, whom she loved but against whose intrusion she maintained a lifelong defence – that must have been bitter, must indeed have been heartbreaking.

Emily could not, would not, stoop to any ignoble feeling about Charlotte's success, but the sensation of Ellis Bell being dragged inextricably in Charlotte Brontë's train was agonizing. Branwell had perished; was the real Emily to perish too? If such an unresolved conflict, unconscious but fierce, was indeed waged in her mind, consumption had a powerful ally.

Anne too felt the unfavourable notices of *Wildfell Hall* very keenly. Her motives in writing that study of drunkenness, performed as a duty and a warning, had been misunderstood and Anne suffered beneath the accusation of enjoying the depiction of debauchery.

It is dangerous to live in Haworth Parsonage and expose one's heart to the hawks of literary London.

SOLITUDE AND SOCIETY

For the next five years Charlotte lived a life of strange and poignant contrasts.

At home in Haworth she experienced an extreme and intense, a really awful solitude. The Parsonage, once lively with six children, was now so quiet that the clock could be heard ticking on the wall. Not only had Charlotte in the past nine months lost dearly loved companions, tied to her by literary creation in common as well as by family affection; she had lost also all companions of her own generation. She lived with her father, now seventy-two, and Tabby who was seventy-eight; Martha Brown was nearer her own age but not suitable as a confidante. Her isolation was complete; hour by hour, day by day, week by week, she had no one to speak to who understood her mind's language. Her casual remark to Mrs Gaskell that the sky became a wonderful companion to anyone living in solitude has a deep pathos; to Ellen Nussey she admitted that in the evening, when dusk fell, her loneliness became often more than she could bear. The boxes of books sent to her from Messrs Smith, Elder and letters from London were the only alleviation to this 'pale blank'; she hung upon the postman's visits with painful expectancy and experienced disappointment almost intolerably keen when he brought her nothing with the London postmark.

The other half of her life was comprised in her visits to London, yearly except in 1852. In London she stayed at

the house of Mrs Smith, mother of George Smith, her
publisher; she visited the Academy, the Opera, received
morning calls from Thackeray (whom she scolded
heartily), breakfasted with Rogers, who had just declined
to be Poet Laureate, sat for her portrait to the fashionable
Richmond, took tea with Harriet Martineau, dined with six
literary critics. Everywhere she went she met people of high
literary attainment who conversed with her as an equal,
people of high worldly standing who desired to lionize her;
everywhere her presence was regarded as an honour.
Smith, who with a sister was fetching a young brother
from school in Scotland in 1850, invited her to accompany
them; she met them in Edinburgh and spent a few golden
days in their company. Sir James Kay-Shuttleworth – the
Lancashire doctor whose reforms and reports inaugurated
the English system of popular education – called with his
wife and invited Charlotte to visit them in Lancashire
and in the Lake District. Luckily Mr Brontë from ambition
insisted on her acceptance, for it was in the Kay-Shuttleworth house by Windermere that she met Mrs Gaskell,
who became her friend and wrote that life of Charlotte
Brontë which is the second finest biography in the English
language.

From these diversions she returned always to home and
duty, to the solitude of Haworth, to Papa's crotchets, to the
silent desolate house and the clock ticking on the wall.
Charlotte suffered from nervousness in all society and
always experienced a certain relief on returning to Haworth.
But the contrast was too violent, the isolation too
overpowering; reaction set in and sank her 'to the
earth'.

Her unhappiness during this period was deepened by three causes: one literary and two of the heart.

Shirley was finished in September 1849 and published on 26 October; it was well received and certainly increased its author's reputation. Charlotte's publishers were naturally eager to 'keep her name before the public' and receive a new novel from her pen for publication in 1851. Mr Brontë too felt this to be highly desirable. But Charlotte, whose grief was revived in the autumn of 1850 by her editing of *Wuthering Heights* and *Agnes Grey* for publication by Smith, Elder and by her composition of the beautiful biographical notice of Emily and Anne which prefaces the edition, had nothing ready. She suggested refurbishing *The Professor* for publication and wrote the preface which we now have, but Smith, Elder advised against the project, whereupon she decided to use some of the material in another form. Smith kindly urged her to take her time over the new novel. Charlotte accepted this with relief, but her haunting fear that her dilatoriness disappointed her Cornhill friends (who could not help inquiring encouragingly about the book occasionally) tormented her throughout the painfully protracted composition of *Villette*. In the winter of 1851–2 she had to lay aside the book for four months during a painful disorder of the liver. During 1852 the 'mood' in which alone she could write often deserted her; conscientiously she vowed to herself not to invite Ellen to stay till the work was finished, but was compelled to break the vow because the misery of continued solitude deprived her of all inspiration. She was not elated with the novel as she wrote it, and may also have felt troubled as to her publisher's reception of a book which undoubtedly portrayed himself and his mother. Meanwhile three years had passed since the appearance of *Shirley*; Messrs Smith, Elder were busy with the score of other writers who had come into notice since Charlotte's first success; letters from London decreased in number; the isolation of Haworth deepened. Perhaps after all she was not a great writer? Her novels were just a flash in the pan? She had always warned Williams of the scantiness of her materials. But she persevered, and in November 1852 *Villette* was finished at last and she said her prayers in thankfulness. Both Williams and Smith received parts of the book with some criticisms; she was paid £500, as for the two earlier books, whereas both she and Papa had hoped for £750; to crown all the bank bill arrived alone, one Saturday morning, without an enclosing letter. She had made up her mind to go to London on Monday to see what had struck Cornhill mute, had not a note from Smith arrived on the Sunday. *Villette* was published in January 1853. The reviews were in general such as to make Charlotte's heart 'swell with thankfulness', but there was of course the usual unfavourable minority (amongst which unfortunately Harriet Martineau's strictures had to be counted), the usual neighbours who always see the bad notices, never the good, and hasten to show what they have seen, with condolences, to the author, the usual misunderstandings of motive and theme; all these matters, pinpricks to the robust nature supported by friends, were sore wounds to the sensitive and lonely Charlotte.

Her loneliness was enhanced by two opportunities of leaving it which seemed to offer themselves. Ellen Nussey declared in later life that George Smith proposed marriage to Charlotte, and certainly Ellen joked about the project in her letters to her friend, calling the pair Jupiter and Venus, and hinting at an undercurrent of feeling between them. Charlotte in her replies, in early 1851, says that there is a liking between herself and the man 'so young, so rising, so hopeful', but that barriers of fortune, convenience and connection of course make any idea of matrimony impossible. An actual proposal seems unlikely, for if Smith had proposed, Charlotte would surely have accepted him. Smith is the original, as we shall see, of Dr John Bretton in *Villette*, for whom poor little Lucy Snowe certainly at one time entertained a passion. But it was a vain passion, and Lucy taught herself to know it was vain and to love instead the irascible M. Paul Emanuel. Teaching oneself that a passion is vain is not very agreeable, however, either in the city of Villette or in Haworth.

M. Paul Emanuel owes much to M. Heger, but something also to Charlotte's other Cornhill lover, James Taylor, a stiff, stubborn, hard-featured, red-haired little Scotsman, a subordinate member of the Smith, Elder firm. In September 1849 he called at Haworth Parsonage on his way back to London from a holiday, ostensibly to take the precious manuscript of *Shirley* up to town, and contrived to make a favourable impression on Mr Brontë. At that time Charlotte hardly knew him, but from then onwards they corresponded on literary subjects, and Taylor regularly sent her the *Athenaeum*. In 1850 we find Mr Brontë in a flutter because 'some overtures' have been made to him about a marriage for Charlotte; these probably came from Taylor, for Mr Brontë knew all about the matter next year without being told, when Taylor came again to Haworth. He was to go to India for five years on behalf of the firm, and came to propose to Charlotte before he left. It is clear from Charlotte's most pathetic letters to Ellen Nussey on the subject that she would like to have accepted him but at the last moment could not bring herself to do so – or perhaps to offer him the encouragement necessary to produce an actual proposal, since she does not clearly record that one was made. He had not enough of the natural gentleman, his mind was second-rate, she could not look up to him, if she accepted him her heart would bleed in pain and humiliation; in a word, when he came near her veins 'ran ice'. Yet his withdrawal left a sad blank; the prospect of a fresh cheerful life which she had begun to entertain had become bitterness and ashes: 'Dear Nell, a more entire crumbling away of a seeming foundation of support and prospect of hope than that which I allude to, can scarcely be realized.' Taylor wrote to Charlotte once before leaving for India, but as it chanced left London a week or two before her yearly visit there. He wrote once or twice again, but only at long intervals and in a tiresomely descriptive style.

When presently, a year later, in the summer of 1852 Ellen asks about India, she hears that all is silent as the grave.

So the thought of Smith was a mirage, and Taylor has disappeared for ever, and Cornhill seems a trifle disappointed in her speed of working, and Mr Brontë has been threatened with an apoplectic stroke, and it even seems wise to give up the book parcels for fear of wearing out Cornhill courtesy; while on the other hand Mrs Gaskell is happily married and has the most delightful children, especially that small sprite Julia.

And so to the Reverend Arthur Bell Nicholls.

MARRIAGE

Arthur Bell Nicholls was born in Ulster of Scottish descent in 1817, being thus a year younger than Charlotte. He came to Haworth, his first curacy, in 1844. His photograph ten years later shows him as quite good-looking, with a long obstinate face, strong features, bright rather staring eyes, and a good deal of black hair and whisker. Conscientious and diligent in parish work, he was a bigot in doctrine; the curate Macarthy in *Shirley*, drawn from him, is represented as unhinged for a week if invited to tea with a Dissenter, and Mrs Gaskell was afraid he would never allow Charlotte to visit with her Unitarian household.

How and when he began to love Charlotte we do not know, but towards the end of 1852 she became conscious of odd behaviour on his part; a constant ardent gaze, a feverish restraint, accompanied by great dejection and frequent threats to leave his post. In December came the proposal; deadly pale, trembling with emotion, in the Parsonage dining-room he asked Charlotte to be his wife. After the manner of the day she inquired whether he had spoken to Mr Brontë; he had not ventured to do so; Charlotte half led, half put him from the house and herself communicated the news to her father. Mr Brontë was furious, and expressed his anger and contempt in terms disgreeable to Charlotte. He was extremely ambitious for his surviving daughter and objected to her throwing herself away upon a curate with only £100 a year; Mr Nicholls had deceived him, and so on. Charlotte's blood boiled with a sense of her father's injustice and she despised his worldly views.

The story of the next six months would be a comedy if it had not such a tragic end. Mr Nicholls would not eat, would not take a service in church, spoke rudely to Papa in public, glared at Martha and behaved very tiresomely with a visiting Bishop; when obliged to officiate at Whitsuntide he broke down on seeing Charlotte at the communion rail and stood white and voiceless while the female congregation sobbed around. Charlotte sometimes felt a poignant pity for his sufferings, sometimes a tart wish that nature had given him the faculty of putting his goodness in a more attractive form. Mr Brontë's continued opposition revealed the strength and fidelity of her suitor's passion so that she could not but respect it, though still regarding him as quite uncongenial. In May, Nicholls threw up his curacy, receiving a gold watch as testimonial from the parish; on calling to deliver some parish papers into Mr Brontë's hands before his departure, he stood so long at the Parsonage gate that Charlotte was obliged to go out to him, and found him sobbing. He went to the south, but soon returned to another Yorkshire curacy, whence he came often to stay with a curate friend in a neighbouring parish. By July he is corresponding with Charlotte, in September he comes to see her, Charlotte tells her father of the correspondence and after a fight wins permission to continue it; in January 1854 he comes again and Charlotte insists on opportunities to know him better; in March she is expecting him shortly at Haworth on quite different conditions; he comes, and by 11 April they are engaged. Her letter to Ellen Nussey announcing the betrothal is surely the saddest which a woman ever penned in such circumstances.

> I am still very calm, very inexpectant. What I taste of happiness is of the soberest order. I trust to love my husband . . . I believe him to be an affectionate, a conscientious, a high-principled man; and if, with all this, I should yield to regrets, that fine talents, congenial tastes and thoughts are not added, it seems to me I should be most presumptuous and thankless.
>
> Providence offers me this destiny. Doubtless then it is the best for me.

Nicholls won Charlotte's hand by loving her only as a woman. He was not in love with Currer Bell, but with Charlotte Brontë. Smith had cared, it seemed, only for the writer, not for the woman; Taylor loved the writer before he knew the woman; Henry Nussey and M. Heger had both admired her mind – for one reason or another all had left her. Now here came Nicholls with his narrow but deep and strong passion for the woman only, and all that was woman in Charlotte responded to it. It was decided that they should live at the Parsonage, and Mr Brontë, whose last curate had been very unsatisfactory, quite welcomed the arrangement.

They were married on the 29th of June that year, at eight o'clock in the morning. One of Nicholls's friends performed the ceremony. Just at bedtime on the 28th, Mr Brontë sent down word that he did not wish to go to Church, so Charlotte was 'given away' by Miss Wooler, with Ellen Nussey for her only bridesmaid. The small delicate figure of Charlotte, in white embroidered muslin, with a white lace mantle and a white bonnet trimmed with green leaves, looked, said the people of Haworth, like a snow-drop. The list of friends to whom wedding cards were to be sent on Charlotte's behalf is most pitifully short — only eighteen in all; she was lonely even at her wedding.

Mr Nicholls and his wife went to Ireland for their honeymoon. While riding through a precipitous Killarney glen, Charlotte was thrown from her horse by a sudden stumble.

Her letters to Ellen Nussey that autumn have a deep though unintended pathos. She knows more of 'the realities of life' than once she did, knows that it is a solemn and strange and perilous thing for a woman to become a wife. Arthur is punctual and practical and likes her to share his occupations; she has very little time to herself and finds her life different from what it used to be. Arthur objects to the frankness of her letters to Ellen; either Ellen must pledge herself to burn her letters, or Arthur will read every line Charlotte writes and elect himself censor of the correspondence. When some pages of a new novel, *Emma*, are read to Arthur, he remarks discouragingly: 'The critics will accuse you of repetition.' Arthur took her out in a thaw through melting snow to see her favourite waterfall; the rain streamed down as they returned and Charlotte caught a cold.

In January, Charlotte was afflicted with perpetually recurring faintness and nausea. Since she was now pregnant, some such symptoms were to be expected and were perhaps not regarded soon enough as serious. The stumble from the horse may have caused internal trouble; perhaps it was the old enemy of the Brontës, tuberculosis, perhaps it was *hyperemesis gravidarum* (excessive sickness of pregnant women) which proved the fatal factor. (Poor old Tabby was taken ill and died while her last surviving nursling lay helpless.) Nicholls nursed his wife with a devotion which she warmly appreciated, but she was not destined ever to make use of the experiences of her marriage in fiction, for she died on the last day of March 1855, leaving her new novel uncompleted.

The publication by Smith, Elder of *The Professor* and of Mrs Gaskell's fine *Life of Charlotte Brontë* in 1857, and Mr Brontë's death in 1861 after long and devoted nursing by his son-in-law, close the Brontë scene.

FACT AND FICTION

The relation of fiction to its source-material in real life is one of deep interest both in its literary and psychological aspects. Henry James gave perhaps the best account of the process when he compared the mind of the novelist to a cauldron of broth simmering on a hot fire. Into this cauldron, as morsels, the novelist throws his real experiences, and when he requires a character, a landscape, an incident, of course he dips into the cauldron and draws one out. But meanwhile the real experience, acted upon by the the heat of the fire and the other ingredients of the broth, has become saturated with the essential stuff of the novelist's mind, has experienced therefore a chemical change, and while retaining something of its original character (like vegetables and meat in a stew) has also undergone a metamorphosis. By this rare alchemy, says James, it is recreated; it ceases to be a thing of fact and becomes a thing of truth.

Thus some experiences, some real facts of life, are essentially necessary for the creation of fiction, and the power to glean experiences is part of the novelist's art; but the greater part of that art is the power of transmuting the real facts into new creations. When the mental broth is comparatively thin and the fire low, the resulting stew is only, so to speak, the thrown-in factual lumps plus water, of which the factual experience alone contains any nourishment. But the hotter the fire, and the thicker the broth — that is, the more powerful the writer's spirit and the richer the composition of his mind — the greater is the transformation.

The Brontës' experiences of actual external life have been recounted; they were few and insignificant, but nevertheless of peculiar mixture and flavour. What their mental powers made of these experiences remains now to be studied. We shall not be surprised to find that the only convincing parts of the mild Anne's fictions are directly traceable to single real originals; that Charlotte's characters and incidents undoubtedly have perceptible originals, but these originals are combined and transformed in more or less degree proportionate to their fictional greatness; that Emily's are from originals so mingled, so fused, so transmuted in her magic crucible as to be for the most part, though the strong wild flavour of their real existences is retained, almost untraceable as individual selves.

Haworth Church and Parsonage, from an engraving, 1857

Charlotte, Emily and Anne with Branwell, from a rough painting by Branwell

Top left: Charlotte writing *Jane Eyre* during the time she was nursing her father, when he was recovering from an operation for a cataract. *Top right*: Anne, from a watercolour by Charlotte. *Bottom*: Haworth Parsonage

Top left: Charlotte, from a painting by J. H. Thompson. *Top right*: Emily, from a painting by Branwell. *Bottom*: Haworth Church

Charlotte, Emily and Anne Brontë from a painting by Branwell

CHAPTER II

The Works of Charlotte Brontë

POEMS

POEMS by Currer, Ellis and Acton Bell, published in 1846, and *Selections from Poems by Ellis and Acton Bell*, edited by Charlotte for publication in 1850, contain only a small part of the verse written by the three Brontë sisters. Careful search and transcription from manuscripts by various editors have now made available some one hundred and fifty-six pieces of Charlotte's, one hundred and ninety-three of Emily's and fifty-eight from Anne. Many of these belong to the Angrian and Gondal cycles, and are written as though proceeding from Angrian or Gondal characters, and dealing with Angrian or Gondal situations.

There is nothing unusual in poetry uttered through the mouth, as it were, of a fictitious character – indeed such poetry abounds in the literature of all nations. The poet (indeed the creative writer of any kind) transfers a real emotion to an imaginary person in order to be able to deal with it fully and truthfully, released from the inhibitions

which would restrict his expression if he exposed the emotion as his own. The Brontës did the same with their
fantasy creations. In Emily's poem *The Absent One*, to
which the date, 17 April 1839, gives the clue, a Gondal
character, R. Gleneden, ostensibly mourns the absence of
his brother Arthur on a battlefield, but really Emily mourns
the absence of Anne, who left Haworth to become a
governess for the first time a week before. This is a crude
example; in other cases the emotion suffers a more subtle
transmutation, but the principle is the same: the poems
express sincere Brontë feelings, though the Brontës never
experienced the fictitious circumstances described.

But there are times when the daydream seizes such hold
on the dreamer's mind that the adventures of the fantasy
characters themselves create emotion in the mind of their
creator. Poems expressing these fantasy feelings, having
their roots in the fantasy world where the operation of
cause and effect is suspended, draw their nourishment only
from fantasy and lack the force and truth of reality. What
strength is there, for example, in the grief of an Angrian
girl over a dead lover when he can be made alive again on
the next page if the Chief Genii desire it? Her grief is valid
only in the Angrian world. A large number of Charlotte's
early poems belong to this valueless category, where the
feelings expressed are essentially artificial and correspond to
no real truth and their expression is a mere literary exercise.

Even in her direct lyrics, however, Charlotte is barely a
minor and certainly not a major poet. She is a capable and
intelligent versifier (on conventional lines) in many metres,
and sometimes produces an ardent phrase, but her verses
have none of that strange overtone, that latent significance,

that moving rhythm, which add up to poetry. Even the verses on the deaths of Emily and Anne, though they must have come from a burning heart, say only what the words say, nothing more. *Rochester's Song to Jane Eyre* is quite lamentable, a tame exercise written (one feels) to order; Rochester himself would have derided its jogtrot commonplace. The Heger poems, *Master and Pupil* (put into *The Professor* as the composition of Frances Henri), *Reason* and *He Saw My Heart's Woe* are well worth reading, not for their poetry but for their revelation of Charlotte's Brussels story, the master's 'mien austere' melting to 'gentle stress', her own 'strong pulse of ambition' and 'secret inward wound'. Her finest poem, *Retrospection*, has but three verses:

> We wove a web in childhood,
> A web of sunny air;
> We dug a spring in infancy
> Of water pure and fair;
>
> We sowed in youth a mustard seed,
> We cut an almond rod;
> We are now grown up to a riper age;
> Are they withered in the sod?
>
> Are they blighted, failed and faded?
> Are they mouldered back to clay?
> For life is darkly shaded,
> And its joys fleet fast away!

On this one occasion, the subject being a fearful question about the Brontë shadow world, Charlotte rises to true poetic expression.

Verse was not, in truth, Charlotte's proper medium. If, however, her poetry is prosaic, there is a fine ardent poetry in her prose.

THE PROFESSOR

Charlotte's four novels form a decided literary unit, to which the fragment *Emma* also belongs; there is emphatically a recurring pattern in Charlotte's literary carpet. As regards their matter: Yorkshire and Brussels, the governess, the tutor and the school are often repeated, interwoven with the cleric and the millowner. In manner a similar recurrence exists, for in all the novels except *Shirley* the story is told in the first person. A deeper unity is achieved by the consistent theme; this is always the conflict between high integrity and worldliness.

It is often alleged that first novels reveal more of their writer's true selves than later works; the truth is probably that they reveal them in a less transmuted and therefore more obvious form. Charlotte employs one bold counterchange transmutation of reality in *The Professor*, by means of which she reveals very plainly her own impressions of her Brussels life; she makes an Englishman play M. Heger's part, a continental play her own, telling the story of the pupil-governess and the adored master through English eyes but from the master's point of view. The professor, William Crimsworth, is the narrator of the tale. The orphaned Crimsworth quarrels with his aristocratic maternal uncles, decides to engage in trade, and becomes clerk to his brother Edward, a tyrannical *nouveau riche* manufacturer in a county which is indubitably Yorkshire.

Through the provocations of a sardonic millowner named Yorke Hunsden (drawn from Mary Taylor's father), William is violently discharged by Edward; Hunsden gives him an introduction in Brussels and William obtains a post as professor in M. Pelet's boys' school there. Presently William secures extra teaching work in a *pensionnat de demoiselles* next door, conducted by the discreet Mlle Zoraïde Reuter; he partly falls in love with Zoraïde, but is disgusted to find that she is already secretly engaged to the insinuating Pelet. Crimsworth is attracted by the neat little needlework teacher, the half Swiss, half English, wholly Protestant Frances Evans Henri, who becomes his pupil for English lessons and reveals taste, intelligence and a heart of fire concealed beneath her demure and reserved exterior. Master and pupil love each other; Zoraïde tries to keep them apart, but eventually they marry, set up school together, achieve a competency and a child and retire to Yorkshire to enjoy them.

The cardinal fact about *The Professor* is revealed by Charlotte herself in the preface she wrote for the abortive project of the novel's publication by Smith, Elder after *Shirley*. She explains that the work was not her first literary attempt:

... in many a crude effort, destroyed almost as soon as composed, I had got over any such taste as I might once have had for ornamented and redundant composition, and come to prefer what was plain and homely. At the same time I had adopted a set of principles on the subject of incident, etc. ...

I said to myself that my hero should work his way through life as I had seen real living men work theirs – that he should

never get a shilling he had not earned – that no sudden turns
should lift him in a moment to wealth and high station ...
that he should not even marry a beautiful girl or a lady of
rank. As Adam's son he should share Adam's doom, and
drain throughout life a mixed and moderate cup of enjoyment. – *The Professor*: Preface

In a word, Charlotte was tired of the glittering tinsel of
Angria, and determined that her story should be as far re-
moved from the land of the Genii and as near to real life as
it could possibly be; its characters should be emphatically
sons of Adam not of Northangerland. Accordingly there is
a realism, an anti-romanticism, in *The Professor* so strong
as to give the book a hue positively saturnine. The characters are drawn in the most determinedly prosaic terms.
When Crimsworth the hero looks in the glass he sees a
thin irregular spectacled face, with sunk dark eyes under a
large square forehead and a complexion destitute of bloom
or attraction. His manners are harsh, his situation obscure;
he is not guiltless of sensual feelings towards Mlle Reuter,
he is subject to hypochondria. The heroine (drawn from
Charlotte herself) is equally moderate in attractions;
'girlish but not striking' is the description Crimsworth
applies to her; shy to the point of gaucherie, she is at first
quite unable to keep order among her pupils. Zoraïde, a
sketch of Madame Heger in youth, and Pelet, are smooth
hypocritical worldlings; their mothers squalid and
moustachioed hags. Of Crimsworth's pupils, the boys
naturally enough are very lightly sketched, but the girls are
full-length portraits of little horrors, presented in a
clinical detail almost worthy of Freud. Even Victor, the

child of Frances and Crimsworth, is described as not at all pretty, but pale and spare, with large eyes.

Charlotte has recorded her own judgement of *The Professor* in her letter to W. S. Williams proposing the re-modelling of the work. She writes:

> I found the beginning very feeble, the whole narrative deficient in incident and in general attractiveness. Yet the middle and later portion of the work, all that relates to Brussels, the Belgian school, etc., is as good as I can write: it contains more pith, more substance, more reality, in my judgment, than much of *Jane Eyre*. It gives, I think, a new view of a grade, an occupation, and a class of characters . . .
>
> – Letter of 14 December 1847

It is a judgement with which today, a hundred years later, we can almost entirely agree. A useful pair of criteria for any work of art is the degree of impression and the kind of impression which it makes upon various minds. There are writers of very considerable narrative power who stamp deep upon the reader's mind impressions which are vulgar, stale or even false; on the other hand there are writers whose views of life have a high nobility and originality, but whose power of impressing them upon the reader is feeble and faint. The great writer is he who makes powerful impresssions of a kind worth making; who offers penetrating analyses and new truths in a fascinating story and commanding words. *The Professor* comes through these tests variously as to its various parts. The early Yorkshire mill scenes are crude in content and overdrawn in style (though even here the landscapes are excellent). The school scenes are truthful, new and powerfully written – good, that is, in both kind and degree of impression,

especially the remarkable contrasted characterization of
integrity and worldliness in Frances and Zoraïde. (Their
masculine counterparts, Crimsworth and Pelet, form a
similar contrast, but are less successfully drawn.) The love
scenes and the marriage, for which Charlotte then lacked
experience, are less satisfying in content and less powerful
in impression. The whole (as she says) is somewhat defi-
cient in incident, and (as we feel) rather too determinedly
drab to be either absolutely interesting or absolutely truthful. But as a first novel it is a singularly original and
powerful production.

As we know, the book was refused six times, and in her
preface Charlotte amusingly explains the reasons for these
rejections. Businessmen are usually thought, she says, to
prefer the real, but she has found this to be a mistaken
notion; they prefer, it seems, something more sentimental,
pathetic and tender, something wild and thrilling, even
harrowing. It is clear that the publishers found the un-
mitigated realism of *The Professor* too strong a draught for
their Victorian gullets. Whether their comments inspired
Charlotte to a more romantic story, or whether, as is more
likely, they encouraged her to continue a story already
begun, we do not know; but certainly her next novel was
her most romantic (and in the opinion of a century her
most successful), the 'autobiography' *Jane Eyre*.

JANE EYRE

The story of *Jane Eyre*, told in the first person by Jane herself, falls into seven well-defined periods marked by
changes of scene. There is the orphan Jane's persecuted

childhood with her relations by marriage, the Reeds, at
Gateshead Hall; her hard, wretched girlhood at Lowood
School, mitigated by friendship and the eager desire to
learn; her governessing of the little love-child Adèle Varens
at Mr Rochester's mansion, Thornfield, and gradual in-
volvement in the mystery of its strange inhabitant; a brief
interlude at Gateshead for her aunt's death, to indicate the
deserved misery of the Reeds and give Jane the address of
her Eyre uncle overseas; her return to Thornfield, leading
to Rochester's bigamous proposal and their wedding, interrupted by the announcement of the existence of his lunatic
first wife, which has been brought about by Jane's letter to
her uncle; then Jane's flight from Thornfield and her stay at
Moor House with the Rivers, who want her to marry St John
Rivers and become with him a missionary in the East, even
when she inherits a substantial sum from her uncle; finally
Jane's seeking out of Rochester, now widowed by a fire and
living at the gloomy Ferndean Manor, and their marriage.

Jane is a version of Charlotte herself, her sufferings at
Lowood are a version of Charlotte's sufferings at Cowan
Bridge School, Jane's friend Helen Burns is a version of
Charlotte's elder sister Maria Brontë. Jane's miseries during
the luxurious house-party at Thornfield are a version of
Charlotte's while governessing, and Mr Rochester is
another version of M. Heger, the strong, stern, sophisti-
cated, dominating master-type. But they have all suffered a
sea-change, a transmutation at once vivifying and colour-
ful; they have been steeped in the glowing hues, the rich
juices, of that romantic faculty from which sprang Zamorna
and Northangerland – a faculty most carefully excluded
when *The Professor* was created. In this process they have

ceased to be things of fact and become things of truth; that is, they have become representative, typical, symbolic, of many facts; they have gained universality by entering the realm of fiction.

The story of *Jane Eyre* is a romantic story. Indeed it appears at first sight the old, old story of Cinderella, or of King Cophetua and the beggar-maid – the story, perennially popular because it expresses a natural feminine wish, of the poor though virtuous girl, despised and persecuted by those around her, who triumphs by marrying the rich, powerful husband. It is a wish-fulfilment story, expressing the writer's unconscious desire, with which the reader identifies herself, for a world where such things happen, where they happen, indeed, to her.

Is *Jane Eyre*, then, wish-fulfilment literature, escapist literature? It approaches that glamorous abyss, hovers on the verge of its illusory depths – but then, resolutely turns away and soars aloft on two very strong and decided wings. That turning away is of immense significance in the moral values of this novel, that is, in the kind of impression it strives to make upon the reader.

One of the factors which saves *Jane Eyre* from being escape literature is the ending of the story. Escape literature always allows the character who represents the fixation of the author's desire to triumph in the end. Now, in the end Jane does not triumph in the worldly sense; she is married to a semi-blind, mutilated man, a man with an inconvenient illegitimate daughter, a man who has earned the just censure of the world and is living in a narrow retirement. If Charlotte had allowed Rochester to recover his sight and Adèle to die off, if the book had closed with Jane appearing in white satin at a ball and being hailed as a dashing beauty, *Jane Eyre* would have been merely a very well-written specimen of a conventional melodrama. But in the last chapter Rochester 'cannot see very distinctly' and Adèle is very much alive; the falsity of the roseate ending, of happiness unmodified by reality, has been avoided; Jane and Rochester drink a mixed and moderate, and therefore real, cup of enjoyment. The union of this honest realism with the highly exciting story makes *Jane Eyre* a remarkable example of that truth-through-beauty which is the function of the novelist's art.

The other factor which wings the book aloft is the superb characterization, which displays this same regard for truth, for the difficult complexity of life as opposed to the false simplicity of melodrama. Observe the admirable minor characters, compound of mingled good and evil as they would be in life: Mrs Fairfax the housekeeper, so good, so simple, so boringly incapable of understanding the mildest joke; Adèle, a silly little butterfly yet loving and lovable; Helen Burns, untidy, unpunctual in spite of her patient resignation and admirable brain; the chilly prig St John Rivers, so noble yet so impossible to marry; Bessie the nursemaid, both quick-tempered and kind. (The rich Ingrams are less successful; for them the essential morsels of real experience were missing from Charlotte's cauldron.) Rochester himself is saved from being a mere hero of melodrama by his very real wit, pride, intelligence and ugliness. And of course there is Jane.

The character of Jane Eyre is Charlotte Brontë's finest achievement. Outwardly Jane is – and remains – a poor, obscure, inexperienced little governess, in neat but quaint

clothes, with pale irregular features, eyes she flatly calls
green, five shillings in her pocket and no worldly importance whatsoever. Inwardly Jane is a 'resolute, wild, free
thing', a 'soul made of fire, a character that bends but does
not break'. When Rochester asks her if she thinks him
handsome, Jane raps out smartly: 'No, sir!' When her
employer commands her to entertain him by talking, Jane
instead of speaking smiles, 'and not a very complacent or
submissive smile, either'. Jane loves Rochester with a
strong, fierce, passionate love – the love scenes in the moonlit garden are exquisitely beautiful – but when thwarted in
this love she commands herself firmly: 'No snivel!' When
begged to become Rochester's mistress, Jane reflects that
nobody would care if she did – and corrects herself immediately: '*I* care for myself! The more solitary, the more
friendless, the more unsustained I am, the more I will
respect myself.' Well might Rochester explain of her:
'Never was anything so frail and so indomitable!' Jane has
'an inward treasure', an integrity of spirit, a fierce rectitude;
in the brief halcyon days of their first engagement, Jane
will not accept handsome presents from Rochester; at
school, her anger over injustice done to another scalds her
cheek with hot tears all day; she cannot live in dependence
but must earn her bread. She has a mind, too; she reads,
she paints, she engages in logical argument, she displays a
biting wit. As she says herself, she is 'a free human being
with an independent will'. She accepts entire responsibility
for her own welfare. In a word, she is the modern emanci-
pated woman – the first in English fiction – struggling with
age-old and basic human problems.

This most strikingly original conception is portrayed in

what Thackeray justly called 'noble English'. Scorning the 'ornamented and redundant', Charlotte uses a plain, strong, essentially *exact* style; her words are intensively expressive of the meaning she intends them to convey, her phrases paint vivid pictures. Her wild moorlands, her candle-lit interiors, her chill dawns, moonlit evenings and lurid midnights, her deathbeds and her dreams, are stamped deep on the reader's mind; her descriptions of the drink-sodden lunatic are truly horrifying.

The kind of impression made by *Jane Eyre* is therefore, though not of the very highest, both original and noble; the degree of impression is exceptionally high.

SHIRLEY

In approaching *Shirley* we cannot do better than take Charlotte's own advice to readers who may be expecting something romantic:

> Calm your expectations ... Something real, cool and solid lies before you; something unromantic as Monday morning.

There is indeed no romance in *Shirley*, though plenty of excitement; it is a real, cool and solid presentation of certain historical events which occurred thirty-seven years before its publication.

The date of the story is 1812, when the effects of the Napoleonic war on British trade are revealing themselves in an almost complete cessation of British exports. From this situation it is well known that England saved herself by the vigorous prosecution of the Industrial Revolution, and Robert Gérard Moore, a West Riding millowner half

Yorkshire half Belgian by birth, is a typical exemplar of this act. The West Riding cloth industry is suffering heavily, bankruptcies among millowners are frequent, unemployment amongst workpeople rife. Moore, a proud and ambitious man, decides to instal some of the just-invented cloth-dressing machines, hoping by the saving in labour which the frames will effect to cheapen his product and expand his market. Some of the local workers, dreading the unemployment the frames will cause, organize themselves in bands known as Luddites, smash these machines as they cross the moor on the way to Hollow's Mill, later attack the mill itself, and presently make an attempt on Moore's life. Moore is supported in his resistance to these attacks by other neighbouring manufacturers, notably Hiram Yorke, and by the clergy and gentry of the district. The gentle and diffident Caroline Helstone, who lives mute and submissive beside her cold clerical uncle, loves Moore, with whom on her mother's side she is distantly connected. She takes lessons from his elderly sister Hortense, and Robert enjoys her company. But Moore's difficulties are greatly increased by the loss of the frames and he believes he cannot afford to indulge himself in returning her love; he proposes instead to improve his finances by marrying an heiress lately come to the district, Shirley Keeldar. The high-spirited Shirley offers to lend him money but rejects his suit; she prefers his brother Louis, a strong stern character who is tutoring one of her young cousins. Thus there is in the book a double master-pupil relationship, for Robert helps Caroline with her arithmetic, and Shirley was Louis's pupil in French in earlier days. Shirley and Caroline become great friends; Shirley's governess Mrs

Pryor proves to be Caroline's long-lost mother. The difficulties in the way of the mutual attachment between Louis and Shirley are overcome by Shirley's frankness, and the termination of the war enables Robert to follow his true inclination and marry Caroline. A trio of curates weave in and out of the action, linking the major characters at useful moments and throwing into relief their natures and situations.

If the main incidents of *Shirley* are historical and the places described real, the characters are likewise factual, being transferred to its pages from real life with little transmutation. Liversedge, the scene of the real Luddite attack on Rawfolds (the original of Hollow's Mill), lies within a couple of miles of Roe Head, and perhaps by unconscious association, perhaps by deliberate choice, Charlotte used many Roe Head characters with little alteration in *Shirley*. In Hiram Yorke and his household are portrayed the father and family of Mary Taylor; Caroline shares some qualities with Ellen Nussey though her soul is Charlotte's; her uncle Helstone comes from an old clergyman of the district; in Mrs Pryor can be recognized many of the harmlessly quaint traits of Miss Wooler; Robert Moore is a mixture of M. Heger and the real owner of Rawfolds. Haworth characters also appear, tinged sometimes with a shade of Brussels; the curates are mirrored direct from life; Hortense Moore is a Belgian teacher mixed with Aunt Branwell; Louis Moore is a mixture of M. Heger and Charlotte herself. Last but most important of all, Shirley Keeldar is said, on Charlotte's own authority, to be a portrait of Emily Brontë as she might have been if rich and free.

On this plane of robust Yorkshire reality, the characterization is admirable throughout, the single case of the priggish Louis Moore excepted. Charlotte's observation of telling detail has never been closer, her range never wider. The minor characters are not only splendidly vigorous portraits in themselves, but, within the limits of the Yorkshire scene, most agreeably diverse, and brightened with many touches of broad humour. Hortense with her ideas on darning and her low view of Yorkshire housewifery is quite *impayable*; Joe Scott the foreman, with his distinction between clean and 'mucky' pride, his confidence in his *métier* and his delightfully laconic account of the Luddites' attack, is a true Yorkshire workman; the timid, ladylike Mrs Pryor, the Sykes and Sympsons – both so vulgar, but in such different ways – the stern Tory Mr Helstone, the old maids Hall and Ainley, the brilliant difficult Yorke children, form a portrait-gallery abundantly various.

Of the major characters, those who remain longest in the memory are Hiram Yorke and the two girls, Caroline and Shirley. Caroline is a most delicate and beautiful study of the girl of her day, the 'young lady' who, cabin'd cribbed and confined by the conventions of the age, if thwarted in a love which she was never allowed to declare was apt to decline and die quietly of a broken heart, crying in silent passion the while for some profession, some trade, some work to fill her head and hands and occupy her thoughts. Being of her age, Caroline is not of all time, and the modern reader cannot but be irritated by her puritanism or masochism, which always rises to forbid her doing or saying the thing which is sensible and pleasant. One cannot love Caroline as one loves Jane Eyre, but one pities her profoundly, not least in her marriage with Robert Moore, whose restless ambitious spirit with its slight mercenary taint is analysed with keen penetration by Charlotte. Hiram Yorke remains to this day the finest extant portrait of the West Riding manufacturer. A rude yet real originality, we are told, is latent in every furrow of his face, but it is an indocile, a scornful and a sarcastic face, the face of a man difficult to lead and impossible to drive. Indeed Yorke, fierce Nonconformist and Radical that he is, cannot endure control; liberty is the breath of life to him, revolt is in his blood. He has travelled much and can speak several languages including good English, when he likes, but he often speaks Yorkshire by choice; one notices with glee that the higher the rank of the person to whom he speaks and the more he dislikes him, the ruder, the racier, the more Yorkshire becomes his tone. In business sagacious and honest, in human relationships he lacks sympathy because he lacks imagination. Shirley tells him that he is truthful, upright and independent, but also harsh, rude, narrow and merciless.

Shirley herself is a very remarkable young woman to find in a novel published in 1849. What such a 'sister of the spotted, bright, quick, fiery leopard' would do in any other fiction of the period, one trembles to think; one spring into the drawing-room with her great dog Tartar at her side would shatter the whole Victorian frame. Lithe, proud and graceful in carriage, frank and free in speech, generous, intelligent and bold in thought, with a clear brow, mobile expressive features, dark hair and clear dark-grey 'she-eagle' eyes, she routs the Sympsons, climbs walls, orders all the provisions in the house to be sent to the soldiers

defending Hollow's Mill, argues with Mr Helstone, and
only falters when she believes herself to have been infected
with hydrophobia by a mad dog's bite. Even so, she had the
courage herself to cauterize the wound. The merit of *Shirley*
is the invention of this fine wild girl; its defect is to allow
her too little scope; she never actually *does* anything equal
to her nature. In the Yorkshire of 1812 there was perhaps
nothing striking for heiresses to do.

In a Verdopolis essay Charlotte defined originality as the
process of raising from obscurity some theme hitherto un-
thought of or despised, and by pouring around it the light
of genius, proving its claim to interest and admiration. In
that sense *Shirley* is strongly original. When Charlotte
began to write it, nobody before had thought of using an
episode of trade, an economic episode, as the main subject
of a fiction. It is true that Charlotte displays no awareness
of the wider sociological implications of the Luddite
episode; still, she raised it from obscurity, thought it worth
using. With its Yorkshire landscape and Yorkshire characters speaking the Yorkshire tongue, enacting Yorkshire
incidents in an exclusively Yorkshire plot, *Shirley* is the
first Yorkshire regional novel. Indeed it is almost the first
English regional novel, Mrs Gaskell's Lancashire *Mary
Barton* appearing in 1848 while *Shirley* was still in process
of composition. *Shirley* is certainly the first *great* English
regional novel, and as such has an historical as well as an
aesthetic importance.

Charlotte's usual theme is less strikingly illustrated in
Shirley than in her other novels. The conflict between
spiritual integrity and self-seeking worldliness is less well
defined, the outlines of the opposing factions are blurred.

Partly this is due to the realism of the character-drawing, no character being represented as unmodified saint or sinner, even Shirley enjoying her rich silk dresses. Partly it is due to Charlotte's too complete acceptance of some of the conventions of her day about women and workmen – for which she was soundly scolded from New Zealand by Mary Taylor.

Shirley is written in a strong, plain, exact style, suitable to the matter described. The writing never reaches the emotional power, never makes the intense impression, found in *Jane Eyre*, and there are some long missish dialogues and diatribes which are frankly tedious. In its best parts, i.e. the Yorkshire passages and the analyses of Caroline's character, it is, however, highly expressive.

If its spiritual content and its emotional tensity are both less than those of *Jane Eyre*, *Shirley* excels in the abundance of life it offers. We are not confined here to the rarefied air of the schoolroom and the drawing-room, or to the society of lonely, hypersensitive and unhappy persons and their opposites of whom they disapprove. Strong turbulent characters are presented in vigorous action, moving about a world which includes roads and mills, woods and fields, curates in uproar, men blue from the dye-vat, Whit-Monday walks and manufacturers talking politics over a bottle, as well as four different households presided over by clearly differentiated women. *Shirley* teems with life – robust, vigorous, outdoor, daylight life, the warm, breathing life of everyday Yorkshire.

VILLETTE AND *EMMA*

When *Villette* was published in 1853 it was received, Mrs
Gaskell tells us, with one burst of acclamation. The public,
who had not then had the opportunity of reading *The
Professor*, found the Belgian school setting strikingly
original and portrayed with a force almost painfully
intense.

The story, told in the first person, is the most compli-
cated attempted by Charlotte Brontë; it is formed by the
interweaving of four groups of persons, each group connected in some way with Lucy Snowe. Mrs Bretton, Lucy's
god-mother, and her son John Graham Bretton, afterwards
a physician; Mr Home, a Scots-French friend of the late
Mr Bretton, and his daughter Paulina Mary; Ginevra
Fanshawe, frivolous, mercenary and beautiful pupil at the
Pensionnat Beck in the city of Villette, and her suitors;
Madame Beck and her cousin M. Paul Emanuel, professor
at the school – these move in a somewhat too artificially
contrived design, in which Lucy makes a strange iridescent
thread. On a girlhood visit to Mrs Bretton, Lucy meets the
little elfin beauty Paulina, and watches the growth of her
adoration for the fickle, careless, vigorous schoolboy John.
Then there is a break in the story; through unexplained
disasters Lucy is left penniless and alone, and presently
decides to seek her fortune abroad. A chance encounter
with Ginevra on the ship, a chance encounter with an
Englishman on the diligence, brings her to Madame Beck's
establishment in Villette; M. Emanuel's opinion of her is
cryptic but favourable, she becomes nursery governess to
the Beck children and later English teacher in the school.

A doctor called to the children proves to be John Bretton, now a suitor of Ginevra and, incidentally, the Englishman who had guided her on her arrival. The Brettons show her kindness; while she is at the theatre with them a rumour of fire causes panic; a young girl is knocked down, Dr John rescues her, she proves to be Paulina Mary Home. After some setting to partners, during which Lucy's 'carnal' love for John causes her great suffering till she conquers it, John marries Paulina, and Ginevra a young military count. M. Emanuel and Lucy are betrothed, and he establishes her in a school of her own to await his return from overseas, whither the jealous Madame Beck has contrived to send him for three years to take charge of a family estate. A fierce storm sweeps the seas when he is due to return; the concluding paragraphs of the book leave his fate uncertain.

It will be seen that there is little creative transmutation in *Villette*; the characters, setting and incidents are taken for the most part direct from Charlotte's experience, from the experience largely of her later years. The master-pupil relationship is portrayed from the pupil's point of view, just as she herself saw it; the appearance, character and behaviour of M. Emanuel, that magnificent-minded, grand-hearted, dear, faulty little man, as she calls him, with a face like that of a black and sallow tiger and a temper to match, were recognized at once by his contemporaries as those of M. Heger. The architecture, situation and educational system of the Beck school resemble exactly those of the Pensionnat Heger, and the mistresses of these two establishments are similarly alike. The fair, compact, neat, able and false Madame Beck with her system of *surveillance*, her spying in list slippers, her reading of other people's letters,

her coldly practical worldly views, was so like Madame
Heger as to make Charlotte anxious to prevent a French
edition of *Villette*. Even Ginevra had a Brussels original,
while George Smith of Smith, Elder recognized himself and
his mother in Dr John and Mrs Bretton, and incidents of
Charlotte's visits to them in London in the fire and other
scenes of the work. Knowing now the story of James
Taylor's proposal, his departure to India for five years and
Charlotte's uncertainty as to his return to her, we understand the reason for M. Emanuel's similar departure and for
Charlotte's refusal to clear up the uncertainty about his
fate. Urged by Mr Brontë to give the book a happy ending,
she herself felt sure that M. Emanuel perished (i.e. that Mr
Taylor would not return to her), but left his death or sur-
vival uncertain so that 'sunny imaginations' might hope.

Charlotte's imagination was not at all sunny while she
was writing *Villette*. Her own life was deeply shadowed at
the time, and the shadow extends itself over the novel,
spreading like a black cloud from the character of Lucy
Snowe. Lucy is, of course, drawn from Charlotte – she even
shares Charlotte's dream-world, speaking of her 'own still
shadow-world' in which she experienced 'the strange
necromantic joys of fancy'. To Lucy, Charlotte, as she re-
marked in a letter to George Smith, was not leniently dis-
posed; one fancies that in her lonely misery it gave her a
grim, bitter satisfaction thus to present herself and her life
in sepia shades. Frankly, Lucy is not an agreeable person to
accompany through a long novel. M. Emanuel discerns fire
beneath her ice, but the spectacle of ice freezing fire is a
chilly one, and Lucy Snowe exudes a frosty breath. The
poor girl suffers from the conviction – so natural to

Charlotte after her repeated tragic bereavements – that Fate is her 'personal foe, never to be conciliated'. 'Dark through the wilderness of this world stretches the way for most of us; equal and steady be our tread; be our cross our banner.' It may be so, and if it be so the courage of endurance is certainly to be admired, but need the way be made darker by a resolute turning from every gleam of sun? Lucy's puritanism, Lucy's masochism, are at times unbearable because so unnecessary. When all the school save herself wear white for Madame's birthday fête, Lucy chooses a crape-like material of purple-grey. When she finds within herself a keen relish for amateur acting which might gift her with a world of delight, she decides that to indulge it would not do for a mere looker-on, and sternly puts the temptation aside. She writes letters to John Bretton in the language of a strongly adherent affection, a rooted and active gratitude – then with a sneer tears them up and writes instead a terse, curt missive of a single page. Longing to forgive M. Emanuel an unkind remark, she tells him instead 'a neat, frosty falsehood' which postpones their reconciliation.

> 'If I feel, may I *never* express?'
> 'Never!' declared Reason.
> – *Villette*, Chapter 21

The exasperated reader can only feel that Lucy's fate is not so much Lucy's personal foe as Lucy's personal creation.

It is not at all necessary, of course, that the main figure of a novel should be 'sympathetic' in order to interest the reader, but it is necessary that the author should be aware

which traits of this main figure's character are genuinely
undesirable. We must not be called on to admire what
deserves not admiration; Lucy is too self-righteous to
please, and Charlotte had no idea that this was Lucy's
failing.

The theme, Charlotte's own familiar theme of integrity
against the world, suffers also on Lucy's account. The
worldlings Madame Beck and Ginevra are properly odious,
the semi-worldling Dr John is (at any rate at first) accurately assessed, the unworldly M. Paul is the darling he
ought to be. But Lucy, who as the critic of worldlings, the
protagonist of truth and honour, liberty and justice, should
be a darling too, an ardent noble soul, is unfortunately a
prig; her cause suffers by her predilection for censorious
gloom.

The truth is that a fault of construction spoils at once
Lucy's story and her character; we are not told what
disasters formed that character, and cannot therefore sympathize with its distortions. If we imagine *Jane Eyre* beginning with a cross little Jane entering Thornfield without a
word about the Reeds and Lowood, we may guess that if
Lucy's early history had been told to us as was Jane's, we
might have liked Lucy better. As it is, Lucy is a failure, and
Villette the least well loved of Charlotte Brontë's three
major novels.

This is a pity, for there are some fine things in *Villette*.
The first part of the work, where that neat, quaint, tiny
child Paulina displays her adoration for her father and her
precocious sexual love for John, is entirely admirable;
closely observed, original, tense and true. (Perhaps the
child Paulina was drawn from Mrs Gaskell's little 'sprite'

Julia, to whom Charlotte in her letters sends very special messages? *Villette* was begun before Charlotte met Julia, but the first chapters of novels are not always finished first.) The whole of Lucy's journey, alone and afraid, from her country home through London to Brussels, is most powerfully written, and so is the account of her sufferings in the school vacation, culminating in that tormented visit to the confessional – though the actual scene with the priest is less telling here than in the account of her own confession which Charlotte wrote to Emily. The character of Madame Beck is superbly drawn, etched in fine lines with the biting acid of hate; M. Paul Emanuel is a thoroughly original contribution to fiction.

It must be admitted, however, that there is padding in *Villette*, that parts of the book seem protracted, laboured. We know that Charlotte found its completion difficult. A possible explanation may be found in the fact that nothing is more tedious to a creative mind than the attempt to recreate material already expended. The meat stewed a second time in the mental cauldron yields little flavour. Charlotte has used the Brussels material once, the master-pupil relationship four times, already; though *Villette* is far more mature, more complete, more powerful than *The Professor* it does not recapture the first fine careless rapture, it lacks the gusto of the first version of the story of Charlotte and M. Heger.

If only Lucy's childhood had been that of Emma! The admirable fragment of that name reveals an ugly unhappy child deposited at school by a rich and distinguished-looking father in a handsome carriage. Her wealth makes her the pet of the worldly headmistress – until Miss

Wilcox's letters to Mr Fitzgibbon are returned by the Post Office, the address given being quite unknown. A quarter's fees for board and education are owing for Matilda, upon whom the infuriated headmistress turns in vulgar rage. The child falls to the floor in fear ... and the fragment ends. One would give much to read Charlotte Brontë's rendering of *père* Fitzgibbon's character, her account of the sensibilities of an honest child faced with such a dishonest situation. Her constant theme would have received, one feels, a new and brilliant illustration.

MERITS AS A NOVELIST

It is not as thinker or poet or social reformer that Charlotte Brontë should be judged. She is essentially a novelist, and as a novelist she merits the warmest praise. She tells a story – and it is always an original story, quite her own – in such a way as to fascinate the reader and convey to him a conviction of its absolute truth; she is fertile in incident, vigorous in narration, vivid in scene. Her prose flies to its mark with an arrow's impetus and precision. Her dialogue is occasionally tedious when her characters intend to be clever, but thoroughly natural and racy when they speak from the heart. Her characterization has great emotional intensity and is sometimes subtle, often strong, always original, always entirely her own. She has created, in Rochester and Jane, two figures of such universally admitted reality that their names now indicate types, recognized categories of human beings. An ardent integrity, an intense scorn for what is base, animates every sentence she wrote. The fire of life burns strongly in her novels.

CHAPTER III

The Works of Emily Brontë

POEMS

ONE of the pleasing testimonies to the nobility of the Brontë sisters' nature is Charlotte's generous appreciation of the work of Emily. Charlotte was the first, indeed during Emily's life almost the only, person to perceive some of the beauty of *Wuthering Heights*, and as we have seen the publication of Emily's poems was due to Charlotte's recognition of their quality. Writing to W. S. Williams in September 1848, when Emily was beginning the decline into her last illness, Charlotte says of her sister's verse:

> Of its startling excellence I am deeply convinced ... The pieces are short, but they are very genuine; they stirred my heart like the sound of a trumpet ... Condensed energy, clearness, finish – strange, strong pathos are their characteristics ...

This tribute is remarkably just as far as it goes, though it neither specifies the two peculiar ingredients of Emily's poetry, the local and the universal, nor analyses its metrical character in any detail. Emily Brontë is a great poet, not only because a sombre and majestic music sounds always through her lines, but because it is a music, so to say, of the spheres, a music of the universe.

> Space-sweeping soul, what sad refrain
> Concludes thy musings once again?
> — *The Philosopher*

Emily's poems are the musings of a space-sweeping soul, that is of a powerful, noble and original mind, whose thought beats on strong wings through the whole cosmos. Emily is also a landscape painter of great power and charm, presenting her unit of moorland earth with equal fidelity and felicity.

Her musings and her descriptions are alike expressed in grave, austere but singularly potent language. Her lines have no bright blossoms of metaphor or simile, and little glitter of epithet; they achieve, however, a wonderful verbal heather-bloom by the never-failing simplicity, strength and exactness of their expressions. Here and there a sudden choice unexpected word — unexpected but recognized when read as inevitable in its stern piercing aptness — gives a patch of brighter purple. Her metres, though moderately varied and handled with easy mastery, are not in any sense unconventional or experimental. But her rhythmic effects are powerful; simple metres, such as the ordinary four-foot and three-foot line in the ordinary four-line ballad stanza, seem to afford her ample scope. One of her rhythms, for example, which occurs so frequently as to

be characteristic and always with magical effect, is the
strong stress on the first foot of the line:

> 'Death! that struck when I was most confiding.'
> 'Vain are the thousand creeds.'
> 'Frown, my haughty sire! Chide, my angry dame!'

Indeed, in their strong surging rhythm the poems resemble
those vast bold sweeps of moorland which Emily loved so
well.

The local element in Emily's poems forms their most
obvious and popular charm. She paints the Yorkshire
moors in every weather, every mood:

> ... in the red fire's cheerful glow
> I think of deep glens, blocked with snow;
> I dream of moor, and misty hill
> Where evening closes dark and chill.
> > — *Faith and Despondency*

> Where the grey flocks in ferny glens are feeding;
> Where the wild wind blows on the mountain side.
> > — *Stanzas*

> For the moors, for the moors, where the short grass
> Like velvet beneath us should lie!
> For the moors, for the moors, where each high pass
> Rose sunny against the clear sky.
> > — *Loud without the wind was roaring*

In all the poems the word *lone*, with its derivatives, is a
key-word, occurring many times, and always with

heart-stirring effect. *And like myself lone, wholly lone – thou lonely dreamer – my lonely years – this summer evening hushed and lone –* the word brings with it all the strange poignant magic that it held for the secret solitary Emily.

Turning to the grand, the universal element in Emily's poetry, we find that in her speculations on the problem of the human soul certain main lines of thought recur. There are several odes – for their grandeur and dignity entitles them to that name – in praise of Imagination, that power 'my slave, my comrade and my king' which made Emily free of a whole shadowy world to roam in. All these poems have an extraordinary potency of expression and a strange metaphysical conception of the imaginative functions. The finest comes from the lips of a Gondal prisoner, who reveals the consolations provided by Imagination:

> He comes with western winds, with evening's wandering
>   airs,
> With that clear dusk of heaven that brings the thickest
>   stars.
> Winds take a pensive tone, and stars a tender fire,
> And visions rise, and change, that kill me with desire.
>
> But, first, a hush of peace – a soundless calm descends;
> The struggle of distress, and fierce impatience ends;
> Mute music soothes my breast – unuttered harmony,
> That I could never dream, till Earth was lost to me.
>
> Then dawns the Invisible; the Unseen its truth reveals;
> My outward sense is gone, my inward essence feels:
> Its wings are almost free – its home, its harbour found,
> Measuring the gulf, it stoops – and dares the final bound.

Oh! dreadful is the check – intense the agony –
When the ear begins to hear, and the eye begins to see;
When the pulse begins to throb, the brain to think again;
The soul to feel the flesh, and the flesh to feel the chain.
                                    – *The Prisoner*

If Gondal and Emily's impulse to defend Gondal gave
us the poems *Plead for Me*, *A Little While*, *To Imagination*,
The Visionary and *The Prisoner*, then Gondal gave us some
of the finest poetry in the English language and we must
be grateful to it and forgive the Brontë daydream habit all
its dire consequences in the lives of the other Brontës.

Another thought which continually animates Emily's
poetry is that of a profound and unjudging compassion for
all created beings. In *How Clear She Shines* we find this wide
charity expressed in a wish that though the earth be
wicked the rest of the universe may remain happy and
good.

> While gazing on the stars that glow
> Above me in that stormless sea,
> I long to hope that all the woe
> Creation knows, is held in thee!
>   – *How Clear She Shines*

The most beautiful expression of Emily's compassion is
contained in the famous *Stanzas to —*. They are clearly
meant for Branwell, though an allusion to his death is a
device of fiction, since the lines were published in 1846.

> Do I despise the timid deer
> Because his limbs are fleet with fear?

> Or, would I mock the wolf's death-howl,
> Because his form is gaunt and foul?
> Or, hear with joy the leveret's cry,
> Because it cannot bravely die?
>
> No! Then above his memory
> Let Pity's heart as tender be;
> Say, 'Earth lie lightly on that breast,
> And, kind Heaven, grant that spirit rest!'

This fine vision, which views the sin and defect clear-eyed, without illusion or palliation, but deeply compassionates the sinner for the nature which fate has given him, is entirely Emily's own; nothing could be further from Charlotte's censorious comment or Anne's pious disapproval. To herself, Emily was severe, scorning the corruption which she believed she found in her own mind.

Courage and freedom are two motives which inspire Emily to a noble ardour. In *The Old Stoic* she reveals her scorn of common aims:

> 'Tis all that I implore;—
> In life and death a chainless soul,
> With courage to endure.

Her finest poem, that strange hymn to the God of Life, begins with the same passionate conviction of the need for courage:

> No coward soul is mine,
> No trembler in the world's storm-troubled sphere:
> I see Heaven's glories shine,
> And Faith shines equal, arming me from Fear.

O God within my breast,
Almighty, ever-present Deity!
Life, that in me has rest
As I, undying Life, have power in Thee!

Vain are the thousand creeds
That move men's hearts: unutterably vain;
Worthless as withered weeds,
Or idlest froth amid the boundless main,

To waken doubt in one
Holding so fast by Thine infinity,
So surely anchored on
The steadfast rock of Immortality.

With wide-embracing love
Thy Spirit animates eternal years,
Pervades and broods above,
Changes, sustains, dissolves, creates, and rears.

Though earth and man were gone,
And suns and universes ceased to be,
And Thou wert left alone,
Every existence would exist in Thee.

There is not room for Death,
Nor atom that his might could render void:
Thou – THOU art Being and Breath,
And what THOU art may never be destroyed.

— *No Coward Soul*

At once practical and mystical, perfectly clear and im-
mensely profound, capable of including the woolly sheep
and the scintillating star in the perception that the God of

Life animates both, Emily's thought is still in advance of the age, still strange, still partly unfathomed, more than a hundred years after her death, while the poetic power, the awful majesty, of her expression in its finest moments has never been surpassed.

WUTHERING HEIGHTS: SETTING AND STRUCTURE

To pass from Emily's poetry to her single fiction is to change neither the rank nor the quality of the work under consideration.

Wuthering Heights is a masterpiece which has been the subject of many ardent eulogies and appreciations almost poetic in their enthusiasm. Indeed a work of art so strange, so wild, so elemental in character requires some poetic fire in the reader to do it justice. It is intended here, however, to subject the book first (however lyrical we may become later) to a calm technical analysis, not with a view to diminish its greatness, but to establish our appreciation of that greatness on the firm base of rational understanding.

First let us observe the wonderful landscape painting, unsurpassed in English fiction. Wuthering Heights is, as everyone knows, the name of a storm-beaten old house on a brow of the West Riding moors, 'wuthering', as Emily explains, being 'a significant provincial adjective, descriptive of the atmospheric tumult to which its station is exposed in stormy weather. Pure, bracing ventilation', continues Emily:

Pure, bracing ventilation they must have up there at all times, indeed: one may guess the power of the north wind blowing over the edge, by the excessive slant of a few stunted firs at the end of the house; and by a range of gaunt thorns all stretching their limbs one way, as if craving alms of the sun.

Magnificently does Emily describe the moors – in winter, when the sky and the sombre hills are mingled in one bitter whirl of wind and suffocating snow and the moor is become a billowy white ocean; in spring, when the larks are singing beneath a blue sky and the becks are all brim full and running with a mellow flow; in summer when the bees are humming dreamily above the purple heather; in the cool of the September evening, when the moths are flutter-ing among the heath and the harebells. The moorland weather, too, is most fully and superbly painted. Scarcely a chapter begins without its indication of the weather – the air was now clear, and still, and cold as impalpable ice; the blast wailed by; a fresh watery afternoon in October; a misty morning, half frost, half drizzle; a golden afternoon of August, shadows and sunshine flitting over the land-scape in rapid succession; a dark evening, threatening thunder; a close, sultry day, devoid of sunshine, but with a sky too dappled and hazy to threaten rain. A great deal of the action takes place out of doors, on the moors, near the sombre towering Penistone Crags, and even when it moves inside Wuthering Heights, the power of the north wind is never far away. The 'house' so-called, into which main room Lockwood finds himself precipitated from the threshold without any introductory lobby or passage, the white-stoned floor, the huge coal fire, the pewter dishes, the oatcake and hanging hams, the painted tea canister, are intensely local in character. The passionate love for

Wuthering Heights felt by Yorkshire people of all types and ages is due largely to this magnificent presentation of the Yorkshire scene.

The plot of *Wuthering Heights* goes as follows. Mr and Mrs Earnshaw, with their children Hindley and Catherine (Cathy), live in a fine old farmhouse in the heart of the West Riding moors, called Wuthering Heights. Mr and Mrs Linton, with their children Edgar and Isabella, live at Thrushcross Grange, an agreeable park-surrounded mansion down in the valley, four miles away. Mr Earnshaw, returning from a business journey to Liverpool, brings with him a homeless boy he has picked up, a dirty, ragged, black-haired, sallow brat speaking a strange tongue, the child perhaps of some Lascar or Spanish sailor. He insists that the waif shall be retained at Wuthering Heights, and gives him the name of a son who had died, Heathcliff, without however adding to this the name of Earnshaw. The story of Heathcliff, as Nelly Dean the Heights maid and later housekeeper explains, is a cuckoo's story. From the first Heathcliff makes bad feeling in the family; Hindley hates Heathcliff and grows to hate his father because Mr Earnshaw loves the intruder; Cathy loves Heathcliff and grows to hate her brother on his account. When Mr Earnshaw dies and Hindley becomes master, he degrades Heathcliff to a servant's level; Cathy resents this bitterly but is not proof against her brother's manoeuvre, she promises to marry the mild and gentle Edgar Linton, and Heathcliff disappears. Some years later he turns up again, rich and outwardly a gentleman. The fearful conflict in Cathy's mind between her love for Heathcliff and her devotion to her husband is too much for her, and she dies when her daughter Catherine is born. Heathcliff sets himself to exact revenge on the Lintons and Earnshaws. He leads Hindley to drink and to gamble away Wuthering Heights to him, so that Hindley's son is degraded to a labourer's standing; he elopes with Isabella Linton, and rejoices that their son, Linton Heathcliff, is Edgar Linton's heir. The wretched weakling Linton Heathcliff is forced by his father to win young Catherine's sympathy, and eventually to entrap her in Wuthering Heights and marry her while Edgar Linton lies dying and unable to make the necessary changes in his will. On Edgar's death and Linton's death, Heathcliff is thus possessed, by right and by force, of all the Linton and Earnshaw property. His plan of revenge is now accomplished, but he is foiled in his wish to make all Lintons and Earnshaws wretched, for Hindley's son Hareton and Catherine love each other and are happy and redeemed by their love. Heathcliff has long been haunted by half-visions of Cathy; he dies when the vision becomes complete.

Not a single item in the above account can be traced to an individual source. The situation of Wuthering Heights is probably that of Withens, an old farmhouse high on the moorland wilds beyond Haworth, but its interior rooms belong to at least two other houses and its richly decorated stone exterior comes from High Sunderland, a seventeenth-century mansion outside Halifax, a mile or two from the school where Emily taught at Law Hill. Penistone Crags resemble the real Ponden Kirk, certainly, but face west instead of east. The characters similarly cannot be traced. It has been suggested that Heathcliff and his revenge come from the *Tales of Hoffmann* and other romantic German

stories which Emily read in Brussels, but since a Gondal
poem *Light up thy Halls*, written by Emily in 1838 four
years before she went to Belgium, applies exactly to
Heathcliff's situation in exile, his resentment and his desire
for revenge, the German stories certainly cannot claim the
honour alone. Irish sources have also been suggested,
while portions of the narrative here and there seem to derive
from certain local Yorkshire tales. Certainly the speech and
actions of the characters are strongly Yorkshire, but no
individual Yorkshire men or women ever claimed to be the
originals of Lintons and Earnshaws. In truth, *Wuthering
Heights* offers a fresh creation; all the constituent elements
have been fused in the fire of genius to form a new, though
symbolic and representative, world.

The structure of *Wuthering Heights* is extremely interesting from the technical point of view. The relationships
described are simple and symmetrical, as will be seen by
the following table:

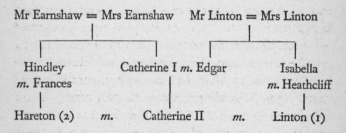

It is but the intermarriages of two families and an inter-
loper, with their consequences; to four Earnshaws add four
Lintons, Hindley's wife and Heathcliff. Three offspring.
cousins, result, and one of them marries the others in turn.

The minor characters are few: Nelly Dean, the labouring man Joseph (that abominable old hypocrite), Zillah the maid, Mr Lockwood, a doctor and a lawyer.

But though the essential facts of the structure are thus simple, the actual building, the actual narrative, is highly complex. Emily employs – as all the Brontë sisters employ in their novels – the first person method of narration. But her story necessarily embraces incidents which could not have been witnessed by the same person. She therefore employs two main narrators to tell the story: Mr Lockwood, who comes as Heathcliff's tenant to Thrushcross Grange in the period between Linton Heathcliff's death and Heathcliff's death, and Nelly Dean, then acting as housekeeper at Thrushcross Grange. Mr Lockwood walks up to Wuthering Heights to see his landlord; a snowstorm compels him to stay the night, he dreams of Cathy Earnshaw and becomes so intrigued by the odd relationships of Heathcliff, Catherine and Hareton that on his return to the Grange he asks Nelly to tell him the story. She complies and with some interludes of discussion with Lockwood brings the long tale up to date. Twice again Lockwood visits the Heights; the second time, after an absence of a year, he sees the happiness of Catherine and Hareton, hears its explanation by Nelly and gazes on Heathcliff's quiet grave. Thus Nelly always relates the past history of the Earnshaw–Linton–Heathcliff families, Lockwood always records his impressions of their present situation. But even two narrators are insufficient; there are scenes in the story at which it is physically impossible for either Nelly or Lockwood to assist. Emily surmounts this difficulty by allowing one of the actors in those scenes – Catherine or

Isabella or the Heights servant Zillah – to tell Nelly about
them, or write a letter to her, or a diary entry which
Lockwood sees; one or other of these main story-tellers is
then able to pass the information thus communicated to
them on to us.

This is a highly complex mode of telling a story. Emily
keeps to it strictly; never are we allowed to know anything
except that which Nelly and Lockwood have seen and
heard. A comparison at once suggests itself with Brown-
ing's *The Ring and the Book*, and another likeness, even
more strong, exists with the work of Conrad, who employs
the 'cloud-of-witnesses' technique with such admirable
effect in *Lord Jim* and other Marlowe stories. There are
obvious disadvantages in the method; it confuses, it
cumbers, it limits, it strains the probabilities – when, for
instance, Isabella relates accurately, in a letter, whole pages
of conversation, we are conscious that in real life she
would not do it so. But there are great advantages too. This
method gives the reader a feeling of intense participation
in the action of the story; is he not hearing about it from
someone who was actually there? The method can, too, be
employed to produce effects of great suspense, excitement,
drama, by means of the very limitations it imposes. When
Lockwood impinges on the Heights story much of it is
already over; he therefore sees and hears such extraordinary
things in that strange house that we are almost mad with
suspense to know their explanation. Nelly Dean begins to
explain, but not until the very last page of her narrative
do we fully understand the situation. When Lockwood
returns a year later and finds the situation changed, he
does not know why and therefore we do not know why;

we are again madly curious to hear the explanation, which slowly drops from Nelly's garrulous lips.

This story-teller method is alleged by some critics to be artificial, but it is in fact completely natural; it is the method by which we hear life-stories in real life. Emily uses it with consummate skill to stimulate our curiosity by communicating an exciting fact without its explanation, not only in the main structure as I have described above, but also to dramatize single incidents. For example: Nelly tells us that Isabella Linton, who so rashly eloped with Heathcliff, suddenly rushed into her brother's house one winter's morning in a thin frock, soaked to the skin, her face bruised and scratched; she was laughing hysterically, quite out of control. Nelly wonders with beating heart what can have happened, and we, listening avidly to Nelly, wonder too. But we have to wait till Isabella tells Nelly. Thus the actual incidents, exciting enough in themselves, have Nelly's suspense and curiosity added to their excitement. The time-shift from present to past and back again similarly heightens the suspense, and gives to the story that romantic glamour, that strange wistful pathos, which Conrad well knew belonged to 'old unhappy far-off things' and so to tales of hearsay.

We may say then that *Wuthering Heights* has a setting grand in itself and superbly presented, and that its plot structure fulfils every demand which can properly be made upon the plot of a novel. The story springs wholly from the conflict of character of the people concerned, as all stories should. From the first introduction of Heathcliff, each happening leads on to the next; the chain of causality is firm and consistent, the march of the action inexorable.

The tale abounds in excitement and suspense, which are skilfully heightened by the peculiar and complex mode of narrative.

WUTHERING HEIGHTS: CHARACTERS AND THEME

The devotion of Yorkshire readers to *Wuthering Heights* was stated to rest largely on its superb presentation of the Yorkshire scene. This devotion is due also to the characters in the book, who are presented with a piercing observation, a strangely mature understanding and an almost terrible intensity. It may surprise some readers to learn that jovial hard-headed robust Yorkshire men and women feel a strong kinship with the sombre and doomed characters of *Wuthering Heights*, but in truth these characters are such as in the secret places of the heart Yorkshire people have often felt they might become – they are the quintessence of Yorkshire, Yorkshire to the *n*th degree, Yorkshire as it might be if it acted without inhibitions in an uninhibiting world.

It is often said that the characters of *Wuthering Heights* are elemental beings; so they are, but none the less they are strongly individual, they are elemental because irrelevant circumstances and characteristics have been refined away and their basic natures, the element which is the core of their soul, has been distilled to its purest essence. In this nature and to the utmost limit of this nature they act, making their own inevitable fate.

Emily shows a remarkable skill in the handling of heredity in the Earnshaw and Linton families. Mr Earnshaw is bluff, hearty, jolly and given to generous impulses; he rescues Heathcliff and overbears his wife's quick vehement objections to keeping the child. He is touchy and easily swayed, likes to be master in his own house and shouts broadly when he is vexed; Heathcliff easily works upon his simple straightforward nature. The picture of him angered against his children and yet loving them and perplexed how all this uncomfortable hatred has got into the house, is piercingly true and pathetic. Hindley and Cathy are unmistakably his children, Hareton is unmistakably his grandson: Hindley the rough hearty fellow spoiled by a boyish resentment which fastens upon his nature like a canker; Hareton warm-hearted, good-looking, with some of his delicate mother's eagerness to be friendly, lost in a difficult world, adoring the man who has ruined him; Cathy the wild and wayward, the haughty headstrong handsome tomboy, light of foot and sweet of smile, always in mischief, torn between loyalty and ambition, rebellious, uncontrollable, passionate and free. So much for the Earnshaws; they are a family, with a strong family likeness; warm-blooded, personable, strong-willed, self-satisfied, they might be any Yorkshire family which let slip conventional controls. The Lintons on the other hand are delicate and thin-blooded, with fair perishable good looks; they believe in gentility, do not farm their land themselves, and are easily downcast by any show of vulgarity or violence. Edgar is good and weak, Isabella is peevish and weak; they love with a clinging love Cathy and Heathcliff, who are so much stronger than themselves. Mingle Lintons and Earnshaws with each other and with Heathcliff's hard cruelty, relentless force and satanic pride. The child of Edgar and Cathy is a young lady, 'the most winning thing that ever brought sunshine into a desolate house'; she is lively and warmhearted but sweet and tender; her spirit is high but not rough; she can be perverse and saucy but relents at one word from her adored father. Under Heathcliff's ill-treatment she turns sullen and defiant, and no wonder; but Edgar's sweet nature triumphs in her and she grows sorry for poor Hareton, teaches him to read and loves him. Again, Linton Heathcliff is complaining, self-pitying, timid, but with cruel impulses which he might indulge if he had strength to pursue them – as he gradually sinks from the mild fretfulness to peevish malignity beneath the pressure of disease and the awful fear of his father he is unmistakably the child of his parents, Heathcliff and Isabella.

There is no character in *Wuthering Heights* who is completely lovable, who wins our sympathy completely. Neither is there any character who is completely odious – not even Heathcliff himself; even in his worst moments we feel for him a kind of sorrowful compassion. Indeed Emily shows to her characters exactly that clear-eyed compassion which she shows when she declines to judge the hare and the deer for timidity, or mock the wolf for his wolfishness. She portrays with absolute fidelity the weakness of the Lintons, the appalling insensate hardness of Heathcliff, the egoism of Cathy and the fatal consequences of all these qualities, yet she views these characters as she does the deer, the wolf and the hare; that is, with regret for their defects, but with understanding and compassion. She deprecates their faults, but does not blame them for their innate qualities or for the development of these qualities beneath the stress of fear or shame; she lets them be heard in their own defence; she shows that Edgar, though a coward, was kind, that Heathcliff, though cruel, was bitterly oppressed.

This just but merciful compassion raises *Wuthering Heights* far above the level of the other Brontë writings. Charlotte and Anne *blame* people for being what they are; they show a strong, personal bias in their animosity against certain types of humanity. Not so Emily. She is able to detach herself from personal prejudice, she is no partisan; anticipating the work of modern psychologists she traces the nature of her characters to its source, understands that nature and rightly values its power for good or ill, its social use or harm, without blaming those who own ill natures for their involuntary possession.

Emily's theme in *Wuthering Heights* is therefore something far deeper and subtler than the conflict of integrity with worldliness. Emily knows the tragedy of the weak good as well as the tragedy of the strong evil; she knows the tragedy of the evil which knows itself to be evil, the good which knows itself to be weak. Her theme may perhaps best be expressed in some words of Conrad, with whom she has certain ideas as well as techniques in common: 'The dark powers, whose real terrors seem always on the verge of triumph, are perpetually foiled by the steadfastness of men.' The dark powers are almost wholly in possession of Heathcliff, and have some lien too on all the other characters; the weakness of the Lintons is due to their paralysing clutch, the vehemence of the Earnshaws to the torment of their claws, while prosaic Nelly, Pharisaic Joseph, time-serving Zillah, mercenary Mr Green the lawyer, have all admitted darkness to a corner of their souls. But these dark powers fall short of their triumph throughout because of that steady human impulse to love one's fellow-men, which all the characters feel in more or less degree; Heathcliff's revenge is foiled at last when he has the children of his enemies completely in his power, because he and Catherine both love Hareton Earnshaw.

WUTHERING HEIGHTS: APPRECIATION

All this might be said of a novel and yet it would not be *Wuthering Heights* and a masterpiece. There remains to be appreciated the degree of impression the book produces, which is terrific, and the quality of the impression produced – which is so wild, so fierce, so dark, so strange and so completely of itself that nothing like it is offered by any other novel in English literature.

The extraordinary degree of impression made on the reader is caused by the intensity of the emotions portrayed and by the terrible power of the words – wild as the north wind, dark as the storm-cloud, strong as the rock, poetic not by their colour but by their force – in which these emotions are recounted. Here for example is Lockwood asleep at Wuthering Heights, dreaming of the dead Catherine. A fir-bough taps teasingly at the lattice.

'I must stop it, nevertheless!' I muttered, knocking my knuckles through the glass, and stretching out an arm to seize the importunate branch; instead of which, my fingers closed on the fingers of a little, ice-cold hand! The intense horror of nightmare came over me; I tried to draw back my arm, but the hand clung to it, and a most melancholy voice sobbed, 'Let me in – let me in!' . . . As it spoke, I discerned, obscurely, a child's face looking through the window. Terror made me cruel; and, finding it useless to attempt shaking the creature off, I pulled its wrist on to the broken pane, and rubbed it to and fro till the blood ran down and soaked the bedclothes; still it wailed, 'Let me in!' and maintained its tenacious grip, almost maddening me with fear ... 'Begone!' I shouted. 'I'll never let you in, not if you beg for twenty years.' 'It is twenty years,' mourned the voice. 'I've been a waif for twenty years!'

The words composing those sentences are not elaborate or glittering, they are simple, even bare and plain; but they are so exactly expressive of such a force of feeling and arranged in so potent a rhythm, that the passage is almost unbearable in its intensity.

The quality of the impression made by *Wuthering Heights* is, like that of Emily's poetry, a compound of the local and the universal. We are alone on the moors, amid the vast heathery slopes, the strong dark rocks, the cold and swiftly tumbling becks, with the wild blast of the wind wailing and raging above our heads – that is, we are alone with earth in one of her grand, wild and sombre manifestations. Presently we encounter persons who have the courage to dare all for a violent, an all-pervading, an overwhelming emotion. The mingling of untamed moorland with symbolic human beings acting intensely as themselves without inhibition gives Emily's masterpiece its incomparable air of dark wild stormy freedom.

Wuthering Heights does not, I think, provide the Aristotelian purgation of the emotions by pity and terror. Its stern story does not move us to these warm human emotions. Rather we feel raised to the level of sombre grandeur and intensity which the book displays; we feel set free, it is true, in body, soul and spirit – but free not from ourselves, only to be more of whatever of grandeur our selves have to offer. What we receive from *Wuthering Heights* is a strengthening of our spirit, our vital core, through an austere contemplation of the quintessence of life which teaches us understanding and courage.

CHAPTER IV

The Works of Anne Brontë

POEMS

ALTHOUGH the verses and fictions of Anne Brontë are the weakest of the Brontë productions, and although they are drawn from some experiences similar to those of Charlotte and Emily and share some of the qualities of her sisters' works, they are by no means a mere imitation of theirs, a mere fainter impression of the same pattern. Anne's material and her mental tone are her own.

Her verses, though sustained above the level of bathos by competent versification and genuine feeling, have no real poetic merit and are chiefly of interest as revealing the nature of this chosen material and this mental tone. The pieces fall into a few main categories. There are long narrative poems in the characters of female Gondal characters, tedious except for occasional references to the Haworth moors. There are some truly pathetic statements of the lonely misery of the governess (e.g. *Lines Written at Thorp Green*, *The Bluebell*, *Past Days*, *The Consolation*) and a revelation (*Domestic Peace*) of the agony Branwell's rackety exhibitionism caused his dove-like sister. There are some quiet but heart-wringing laments for the sunny smile and angel-fair form with which the Rev William Weightman had gladdened Anne's heart (*A Reminiscence, Severed and Gone*) and – the largest group – many religious poems of a fervid and most melancholy piety, in which the gentle Anne sought to strengthen her 'trembling soul' and 'feeble faith'. Extracts from some of these religious verses (*A Prayer, The Three Guides*, etc) have been printed in the Baptist and other hymnals. From her poems we perceive that the four great facts of Anne's life were her fervent piety, the loss of her hope of love, her governess experience and her proximity to a drunken brother. In her fictions she etched in faint delicate wistful lines the happiness of winning a clergyman's love, and portrayed the life of the governess and the drunkard with a resigned but relentless truthfulness which she believed to be required of her by the will of God.

AGNES GREY

Agnes Grey is a first-person story, told by the title-character. Agnes, the younger daughter of a clergyman who has lost his patrimony in a sea venture, bravely sallies forth into the world as a children's governess. Her first post is with the Bloomfields, *nouveaux riches* of a coarse unfeeling type; the children are rough, rude and deceitful and she can make no headway with them. (It must be admitted that her methods, viewed from the modern psychological standpoint, could scarcely be worse.) Her sufferings are depicted with appalling vividness; the picture of the unhappy girl wedging Tom into a corner by seating herself before him in a chair, holding the book containing the task to be said or read in her hand and declining to move till he shall have completed it, is unforgettable. Mary Ann, too, has to be forcibly held up with one hand while the other supports the lesson book. The children often decline to say the necessary word which will release them and their hated governess to the garden; they spit into her workbag and threaten to throw her desk out of the window. The parents become dissatisfied and poor Agnes is dismissed. After a short rest at home she again ventures forth, this time to an aristocratic family, the Murrays of Horton Lodge, largely drawn from the Robinsons. Here, after being duly shocked by the manners and morals of high life, she succeeds in gaining the affection and even the (somewhat derisive) respect of her pupils Rosalie and Matilda. She visits the poor and falls in love with the new curate, Mr Weston, who is a serious version of Mr Weightman. A slight estrangement arises between the lovers with the assistance of the coquette Rosalie. Then Agnes's sister marries, her father dies, her mother begins a school at a seaside resort and Agnes must leave Horton Lodge to help her. All is well in the end, however; for while the heartless Rosalie marries the dissipated Sir Thomas Ashby and learns to hate him, Mr Weston is appointed to a parish just outside Agnes's seaside town and after proper preliminaries the lovers are united. The fine description of Scarborough sands in the early morning light has an unintended pathos; no lover came to Anne herself beside that broad bright bay, but only death.

The structure of *Agnes Grey* is very simple; it is a mere relation of a series of small domestic incidents – the chapters are headed 'The Shower', 'The Letter' and so on. Its theme is the struggle of spiritual integrity to hold its own in a difficult world. There are many pages when, with its curate hero and its patient persecuted heroine, its district visiting and shocked comments on flirtation, its pretty pictures of cat and dog and pigeon, the novel seems naïve and weak, fit only for a Sunday School prize for a decidedly junior class.

But there is more in Anne's first novel than that. The keen observation, the frank language, the unsparing honesty of the account of the governess's struggles with her pupils, struggles so unflattering to herself, make the book far too strong meat for such missish palates. Anne's firm avoidance of the sentimental appears with admirably vivifying effect in her descriptions of her characters. Says Agnes of her own appearance: 'I could discover no beauty in those marked features, that pale hollow cheek, and ordinary brown hair; there might be intellect in the forehead, there might be expression in the dark grey eyes, but what of that?' Few are the heroines of fiction equipped with 'ordinary' hair and an intellectual forehead; Agnes becomes a real human being for us at once. Mr Weston's appearance has a similar reality because it is described in terms of the same lifelike moderation, and Sir Thomas Ashby is a real villain, not the handsome sinister type dear to the immature mind, for his face is pale and blotchy, with a disagreeable redness about the eyelids. The crowning example of this convinced and deliberate realism occurs in the replies given by Agnes to Rosalie's questions about her sister's fiancé.

'Is he rich?'
'No; only comfortable.'
'Is he handsome?'
'No; only decent.'
'Young?'
'No; only middling.'

The quiet little governess will never allow herself to romanticize the facts, even in the excitement of a beloved sister's betrothal. Anne's experience did not include M. Heger, and we have no 'beloved master' type in her novels; it is tempting to wonder what her religious realism would have made of the original of Mr Rochester. Studying the character of Huntingdon in *The Tenant of Wildfell Hall*, one fancies she would have deflated that dissipated gentleman, taken him down several pegs.

THE TENANT OF WILDFELL HALL

The structure of *The Tenant of Wildfell Hall* is an interesting one. The book falls into three parts, each part a first-person story. Gilbert Markham, the northern farmer, tells of the coming of Miss Helen Graham to the Hall, of his love for her, of her equivocal situation with regard to a neighbouring estate-owner, Frederick Lawrence, of his attack on Lawrence and the painful scene with Helen which follows. Helen gives him her diary to read; in it she tells the story of her marriage with the roué Arthur Huntingdon and her determination to leave him when she sees that he is beginning to corrupt their little son. She has come to Wildfell Hall to be near her brother Lawrence. Gilbert's letters now again take up the tale. Helen returns to nurse her husband, who has had a hunting accident and dies as a result of his intemperate habits; after a few mild misunderstandings and hesitations on Gilbert's part on account of Helen's fortune, a happy marriage between Helen and Gilbert takes place.

The change of narrator from Gilbert to Helen and back to Gilbert, which at first sight seems clumsy, is in truth necessary to give this particular story its full effect. If we are to feel Helen's attraction and the mystery of her situation at Wildfell Hall we must see that situation through Gilbert's eyes; if we are to appreciate the anguish of Helen's sufferings with her husband, we must see those sufferings through Helen's eyes; but we must see from Gilbert's point of view Helen's access of fortune or we cannot get the full flavour of his scruples. It is not without significance that in each case it is the sufferer who is chosen to tell the tale; Anne understands only too well the feelings of the suffering and oppressed.

The great merit of *Wildfell Hall* is the feature which Charlotte thought a great mistake: its terrible picture of the gradual deterioration of a drunkard. Drawn, of course, from the model close at hand in Haworth Parsonage, the portrait of Arthur Huntingdon convinces in every detail. The very shape of the drunkard's head, with its depressed crown masked by rich curls, his florid complexion and full lips, his 'long low chuckling laugh' when Helen justly accuses him, his sick peevishness after a drinking bout, his essential lightness of head and heart, his soda-water breakfasts and brandy luncheons, his alternate insolence and yearning towards his wife, his boasted infidelities – no other handling of this subject in fiction has exceeded these keenly observed and strongly portrayed details in truth and impressiveness.

It is to Anne's anti-romanticism that we owe the telling of this part of the novel from Helen's point of view. The story of the woman with a brutal husband appears prettiest when seen through the eyes of the hero who meets, pities, loves and rescues her. The agony, in such a story, is sharp but exciting and short. But the real agony of such stories when they occur in real life is that they are monotonous and long; Anne shows this agony faithfully, although it made her wretched to do so.

A point of interest about Anne's two novels is that in subject-matter they do not in the least repeat each other. The suffering heroine of *Wildfell Hall* is not a poor plain governess, but a rich and handsome woman; the only governess introduced is the atrocious Miss Myers, who comes to the Huntingdons' house to carry on an intrigue with its master. The character of Helen while she is Huntingdon's wife is indeed unique in the Brontë repertoire. With intelligence and pride Helen combines beauty and charm; her power of exciting men's love, her resentment as a scorned wife, her indignant repulse of the dishonourable proposal made her by one of Huntingdon's worthless friends and her passionate love for her little boy belong to a view of life more normal than either Emily's or Charlotte's.

PIETY AND REALISM

Anne Brontë's mind, though above the average, was not a genuinely powerful one, her vision was not wide. Naïveté and religiosity make her characterization, outside the limits of real people she had observed, often either feeble or crude, her dialogue tedious, her story slight. But her moor scenes and seascapes, her uncomfortable snowy journeys and desolate arrivals, in fact all her settings and her simple actions, are described in words of considerable expressiveness and strength; her relentless honesty and the close realistic observation it dictated make her worth accompanying when she is dealing with her own peculiar material. It is doubtful whether her novels would be widely remembered today if she were not sister to Emily and Charlotte. But a few readers would always find *Agnes Grey* and *Wildfell Hall* worth reading for the sake of certain aromatic ingredients here and there which impart to the otherwise mild and pious flavour a sudden harsh heathery tang.

CHAPTER V

The Brontës' Place in English Literature

A CENTURY and a quarter have passed since the first Brontë novels were published, years crowded with masterpieces of English fiction. Half the work of Dickens, the best of Thackeray, the novels of Trollope, George Eliot, Meredith, Hardy, Conrad, Galsworthy, Wells, Bennett, Forster, Woolf and Joyce have supervened. Have these writers, with all that they have added and changed in English fiction, outdated the Brontës? Outdating occurs when later work gives what earlier work gives, with additions or improvements which make the earlier appear clumsy or incomplete, in a word less enjoyable than the later, and therefore unnecessary. Is it still worth while to read the Brontë novels? Do they, that is, still give the reader a powerful and unique experience, an experience he can secure from no other fiction? If so, what is this experience? Is it worth having? What is the Brontës' place in English literature?

Perhaps we ought to inquire first whether we have the right to speak of the Brontës as a literary unit. The analysis in the preceding pages has indicated that their work is less homogeneous than is sometimes supposed. Charlotte had, so to say, a more worldly, in the sense of more outwardly turned, mind than her sisters; she was active, aspiring, capable of culture (i.e. of learning by contact with other minds), and had sturdy sexual passions. Normal happy family life is never the basis of her fictions, for the family household is too circumscribed a sphere for her ambitious spirit. Her strong and ardent feeling for the romantic was however continually repressed by her Victorian puritanism, which at times bordered on the masochistic. How often we read in her letters that she is schooling herself against the anticipation of any pleasure, that she prays for strength to resist the lure of pleasure, that she even thinks of giving up the stimulus of her London correspondence because 'temporary excitement' can do no 'real good'! To Charlotte duty was paramount, and what was pleasant, except in Angria, could not be duty. It followed that those who led pleasant carefree lives – for example, the rich and worldly – must be neglecting their duty and should be condemned. Her censorious comment is the measure of her unconscious longing, sternly chastised and strongly suppressed.

Anne shares this self-denying ordinance, but to her it has been dictated by a stern though loving God.

Emily, altogether free of such vain creeds, views humanity from a point of view beyond the stars, like Hardy's Chorus of the Pities, and feels like them an impartial justice, an austere compassion.

Yet in spite of these differences the three sisters have much in common. All write terse, simple, expressive prose, classic in its lack of redundant ornament, its neglect of temporary fashion. Through this prose in its best passages sound strains of a certain wild music peculiar to the Brontës, a compound of the moorland and the Mourne. All use a clear, downright and exact mode of relation, as if too scornful to attempt to attract by any dissimulating frill. All make much use of the first-person narrative – though Charlotte and Anne use it only for persons with whom they sympathize, while Emily extends it to the peevish, the surly and the conceited. All have a passion for truth which is accurately described in the words of Lucy Snowe as literal, ardent, bitter. All three Brontës write of the adventures of the spirit; no mere material success ever contents the persons of their novels. Jane, rich in her legacy, thinks herself poor in happiness till she finds the blinded Rochester; Agnes Grey scorns the lovely Rosalie for her successful marriage of ambition; it is when Heathcliff is most powerful in the worldly sense that in Emily's sense he is defeated. All the Brontës admire courage, admire the indomitable character making his (or her) way through the world with undaunted persistence; all admire the true pride of work and despise the false pride of dependence; all hate tyranny, despise ostentation and love freedom. All have a great ardour of soul, a terrible intensity of feeling.

There is thus a family likeness in their genius, which yet is individual and produces individual creations. All the cells of a plant draw their life from the same earth, air and sun, but by functional modification they assume widely differing appearances and duties, becoming root, stem, leaf, calyx, petals, stamens, pistil. Of such a plant we might consider Charlotte's work the abundant and brilliant leafage, Emily's the single strangely shaped deep purple flower (fruitful, magnificent), while Anne's must be allotted the humbler identity of bract or sepals, protecting the blossom but of less strength and beauty and sooner withering away. It seems legitimate to consider the Brontë productions as a whole, provided these differences be remembered.

What, then, is the nature of this Brontë contribution to literature?

Their most obvious contribution is, of course, their presentation of that unit of northern earth known as the West Riding of Yorkshire. They all present its landscape – Charlotte realistically, Anne nostalgically, Emily fully, poetically, superbly. They all use its rich rough dialect. Charlotte presents a vital moment of its history. They all present its people – though they present them in three different ways. In *Wuthering Heights* the Yorkshire character is presented in quintessence, as though all the wilful Yorkshire lasses who ever lived had been distilled into the wilfulness of Cathy. In *Shirley* the Yorkshire character is shown to us realistically and consciously. Charlotte there meant her picture to be definitely and recognizably the West Riding of 1812; the background of the cloth trade, the Whitsuntide school treat, the Yorkshire speech, the rendering of Yorkshire character in Joe Scott and Mr and Mrs Yorke – all this is a deliberate (and entirely successful) attempt to sketch the Yorkshire scene. Lastly, Charlotte and Anne Brontë present the northern character to us, *unconsciously*, in their portraits of the poor proud little governesses: Jane Eyre, Agnes Grey, Frances Henri, Lucy Snowe. These were not intended by their authors to be particularly Yorkshire, but in fact they represent some of the basic characteristics of the northern woman in a highly significant way. These little governesses (self-portraits, of course, with the genius left out) are not pretty, not elegant, not what a later Yorkshire author has called 'la-di-da', not in any sense women of the world; in truth they are somewhat obstinately and unrepentantly provincial. So – if I may as a Yorkshirewoman be forgiven for saying this – so are many Yorkshirewomen. But these governesses have also that stubborn unbowed independence, that innate sense of equality with all the rest of the world, which is the heritage of the northern English people. Compare these governesses with the helpless vapid heroines of Dickens and Thackeray, the fine but chained women of George Eliot, the sheltered ladies of Trollope, the captives struggling in a glittering net of Meredith, the doomed life-conduits of Hardy, the persecuted victims of Galsworthy – the contrast is certainly striking; the Brontë heroines are women with a brain and a backbone and a pair of useful hands; women not to be found again in English literature until the north-midland industrial fictions of Arnold Bennett; they are northern women.

The melancholy, the poetry, the fire and ice of these fictional governesses comes, of course, from the other side of the Brontë nature, from their Irish heritage.

For there is a peculiar quality in the Brontë presentation of Yorkshire: a quality of wild poetry, of arrogance, of melancholy, of stormy intransigence and fiery intensity, of passionate scorn for material values, which is not native to that robust and practical county. This is the Celtic strain, which mingles with the Yorkshire to produce so strange a blend. There are no other Yorkshire writers like the Brontës, for all other Yorkshire writers hitherto lack the

Celtic strain. There are no other Irish writers like the
Brontës, for all other Irish writers hitherto lack the Yorkshire strain. The experience the Brontë novels offer to the
reader is therefore still unique.

It is tempting to sum up the Brontë sisters as speaking
Irish poetry in a Yorkshire accent. But that is not quite
true. Rather is their matter Yorkshire, their manner Celtic.
Let us say then that their work is a Yorkshire tune played
on an Irish harp by varyingly strong and skilful fingers. To
this tune Charlotte adds passionate, Anne pious and Emily
cosmic harmonies.

SOME BOOKS ABOUT THE BRONTËS

THE SHAKESPEARE HEAD BRONTË. (*Novels*, 11 vols; *Lives and Letters*, 4 vols; *Poems of E. & A. Brontë*, 1 vol; *Poems of Charlotte Brontë*, 1 vol; *Miscellaneous and Unpublished Writings of Charlotte and Patrick Branwell Brontë*, 2 vols. Edited by Wise and Symington. Blackwell, 1934–8.)

BENTLEY, PHYLLIS. *The Brontës and their World*. (Thames & Hudson, 1969.)

DIMNET, ERNEST. *The Brontë Sisters*. (Translated from French. Cape, 1927.)

GASKELL, Mrs E. C. *The Life of Charlotte Brontë*. (Smith, Elder, 1857. Everyman, 1908.)

GÉRIN, WINIFRED.
Anne Brontë. (Nelson, 1959);
Branwell Brontë. (Nelson, 1961);
Charlotte Brontë. (Clarendon Press, 1967);
Emily Brontë. (Clarendon Press, 1971).

LANE, MARGARET. *The Brontë Story*. (Heinemann, 1953.)

LOCK, J. and DIXON, W. T. *A Man of Sorrow* (Rev P. Brontë). (Nelson, 1965.)

RATCHFORD, FANNIE ELIZABETH. *The Brontës' Web of Childhood*. (Columbia University Press, New York, 1941.)

ROBINSON, A. MARY F. *Emily Brontë*. (Allen & Co, 1889.)

SHORTER, CLEMENT. *The Brontës: Life and Letters*. (2 vols. Hodder and Stoughton, 1908.)

WROOT, HERBERT E. *Sources of Charlotte Brontë's Novels: Persons and Places*. (Publications of the Brontë Society, 1935.)

Charlotte Brontë

JANE EYRE　　　　　　　　　　30p
Introduction and Notes by Storm Jameson

This story of the homely orphan governess who
wtns the heart of Mr Rochester, her apparently
heartless employer, is one of the world's
greatest love stories – as convincing today as
when it first appeared.

VILLETTE　　　　　　　　　　40p
Introduction and Notes by Gilbert Phelps

Charlotte Brontë's last novel, *Villette*, fully and
brilliantly expresses the theme she had attempted in her first, *The Professor*, and shows the
culmination of her genius in relating personal
experience to its social and psychological
implications. For both novels are based on her
own experience as a teacher in Brussels and
reflect her own unrequited love for her employer, Monsieur Heger.

These and other PAN Books are obtainable
from all booksellers and newsagents. If you
have any difficulty please send purchase price
plus 7p postage to PO Box 11, Falmouth,
Cornwall.
While every effort is made to keep prices low, it
is sometimes necessary to increase prices at
short notice. PAN Books reserve the right to
show new retail prices on covers which may
differ from those advertised in the text or
elsewhere.